FAQ
PSYCHOANALYSIS

HIMANSHU VAIDYA

a wise man is free even from his own ideas - Lao Tzu

Preface

FAQ is an attempt to popularize knowledge, make it easy and delicious. It is a series of books on a variety of subjects and this on Psychoanalysis being the first in the series. The FAQ series addresses the desire of many, who want to read on a variety of subjects like Psychoanalysis, Philosophy, Management and Religion but who find the existing scholarly books too difficult. FAQ series offers knowledge in a simple format of short questions through which the reader is initiated into an otherwise complex subject.

The FAQ series in no way competes with the scholarly books. It aspires to initiate readers into subjects of their interest expecting the reader so initiated continues his journey deeper into the subjects. The FAQ series begins with this work on Psychoanalysis and in future shall engage with subjects viz. Philosophy, Spirituality, Management, Non-Profit Management, Social Marketing, Brand Management, Marketing, Consumer Behavior, Fashion Marketing and Corporate Social Responsibility. The FAQ series shall be available in the e-book and classical book form.

This book deals with the subject of Psychoanalysis and it provides a general perspective and an entry into seven important Psychoanalytic schools. Each school is explained in one chapter and the title of the respective chapter is same as the name of the founding father of the said school. The book covers seven important schools in Psychoanalysis founded (one each) by Sigmund Freud, Carl Jung, Melanie Klein, Donald Winnicott, Heinz Kohut and Habib Devanloo. Some important psychoanalysts like Lacan, Alfred Adler, Erik Erickson, Fairbairn and others have not been included owing to a variety of reasons including; my own limitations of knowledge, in some cases my lack of belief in validity of what they said, and in a few cases the fact that they are no longer are so popular in practice. Even with such selection the book truly provides a perspective on Psychoanalysis.

If some readers end up becoming analysts beginning here or if a practicing therapist finds his practice enriched or if a reader feels enriched, the work shall stand rewarded.

I hope this book fulfills the purpose of popularizing knowledge, making knowledge delicious and learning distanced from fear, and that it draws ever more people into a conversation called reading.

Index

What is Psychoanalysis?

the journey of a thousand miles has to begin with a single step - Lao Tzu

1.When did Psychoanalysis come into existence and what is it?

Psychoanalysis is an area within Psychology. Psychoanalysis was founded by Dr. Sigmund Freud about 100 years ago (in 1886 to be exact Freud started his private practice after which Psychoanalysis slowly emerged). Psychoanalysis believes in the existence of the unconscious mind and it is this belief that sets Psychoanalysis apart from most approaches and schools within Psychology.

2.What are the fundamental beliefs on which Psychoanalysis rests?

Psychoanalysis believes in the following axioms and these beliefs have come out of self-analysis of psychoanalysts as well as analysis of patients,

1) Existence of the unconscious mind
2) The unconscious mind governing a major part of our mental life
3) Psychopathology being rooted in the unconscious mind
4) The co-existence of reality and fantasy in the psyche.
   What it means is that the human mind is engaged with both reality and fantasy. No man has a fantasy free mind nor is there a man who is a logic machine
5) Psychic determinism governing mental functioning, which means that there is a reason or motivation for every mental activity
6) Health and Pathology being on a continuum.
   What it means is that pathology is an exaggeration of normalcy and there is no unbridgeable gulf between pathology and normalcy. For example, a person who is paranoid has excessive fear and that doesn't mean that a normal person has no fear. It is just that the paranoid person suffers from an exaggeration of fear.
7) Primary of childhood, i.e. before the age of 7 much of the foundation of our mind as well as roots of our psycho-pathology and health are already in place
8) Significance of dreams, slips of tongue, slips in writing and free association
   Since these things provide us an opening into the unconscious mind

3   What is Psychoanalytic Psychotherapy?

Psychoanalysis is a body of knowledge which has its understanding of how the mind functions, how pathology develops and how healing can happen. Psychotherapy which is based upon (the knowledge of) Psychoanalysis is called Psychoanalytic Psychotherapy. Just as there are other forms of Psychotherapy like Cognitive Behavioral Therapy, Rational Emotive therapy, Logo therapy (there are more than 50 approaches in the area of Psychotherapy) Psychoanalytic Psychotherapy is one form of Psychotherapy based on the knowledge of Psychoanalysis.

Psychoanalytic Psychotherapy should be practiced only by a person especially trained in Psychoanalytic Psychotherapy and not by anyone who has just done a general post-graduation in Clinical Psychology.

4. What is the difference between Psychoanalysis and Psychoanalytic Psychotherapy?

A person who comes into Psychoanalysis with a problem to heal is coming for Psychoanalytic Psychotherapy whereas a person who comes only to know himself better and not to heal any psychological problem is coming for Psychoanalysis.

The focus in Psychoanalysis is to arrive at how the mind works, especially involving thoughts, feelings, beliefs and unconscious templates. The focus of Psychoanalytic Psychotherapy is to heal the problem for which the person has come and so the 'focus on healing' becomes a critical factor.

5. What is a Complex? How is it involved in Psychopathology? How does healing happen?

Complex is a mental entity that consists of two things Idea and Affect (feelings). The Idea is 'loaded' with affect.

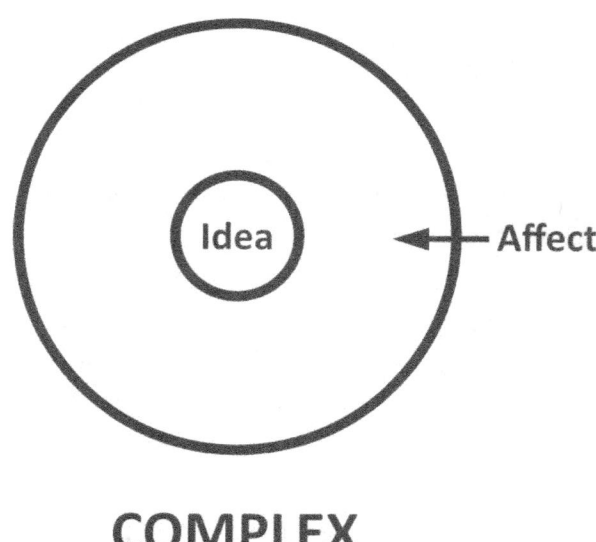

COMPLEX

The Complex when it is in the unconscious exerts strong influence on the mind and is also responsible for Psychopathology. Say for example, as an infant during the rainy season when thundering happens, the infant is terrified of the thundering sound and he associates thundering with rains (since he is unable to understand the real mechanism of thundering). Hence a Complex develops here where the Idea of rains is loaded with the affect (feeling) of fear. As an adult the person start feeling anxiety whenever he sees rains or clouds. The person is unable to find any conscious reason for such anxiety because the cause 'the Complex' is in the unconscious where the Idea of rains is associated with fear. Unless the person goes into therapy it is very difficult to overcome one's Complexes which are in the unconscious mind.

Healing happens when the Complex comes into awareness through the process of therapy. The conscious mind comes to know of the Idea part of the Complex and the affect part of the Complex gets free from the Idea and is then available for constructive mental functioning. In our example when the person as an adult comes to realize that this infantile template was created when as an infant he felt his survival was in danger owing to the thundering sound and hence extreme fear was aroused. Now as an adult that he knows that his survival is not in danger and he understands the mechanism of rains and thundering, he develops an 'insight' that the association of rains with thundering and of thundering to danger of survival is an infantile understanding without any basis and as an adult he is safe there is no danger to his survival from rains or thundering.

Once he develops the above insight two things happen. The unconscious idea of rains being linked to thundering being linked to danger to survival becomes conscious and the affect (feeling) of fear linked to the idea is set free from the idea. With this healing happens.

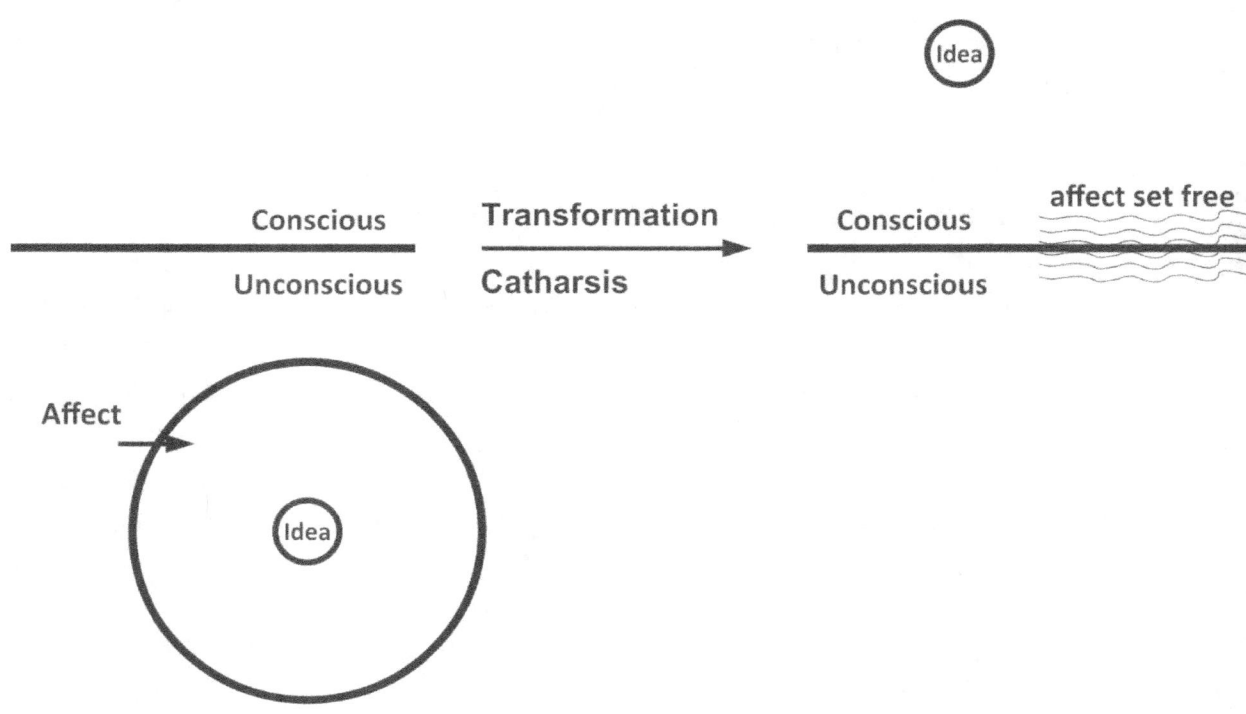

THE PROCESS OF HEALING

Thus getting the Idea into awareness and setting free the affect which was loaded on the Idea are both important from healing point of view. If the Idea gets known but the affect is not released free then often it happens that the affect gets detached from the Idea and gets attached to another idea in the unconscious creating a new Complex in the unconscious. Because of this often symptoms change like a person who was washing hands 20 times a day now starts checking locks 20 times a day if he has locked it properly. Thus free release of affect is extremely important in Psychoanalytic Psychotherapy.

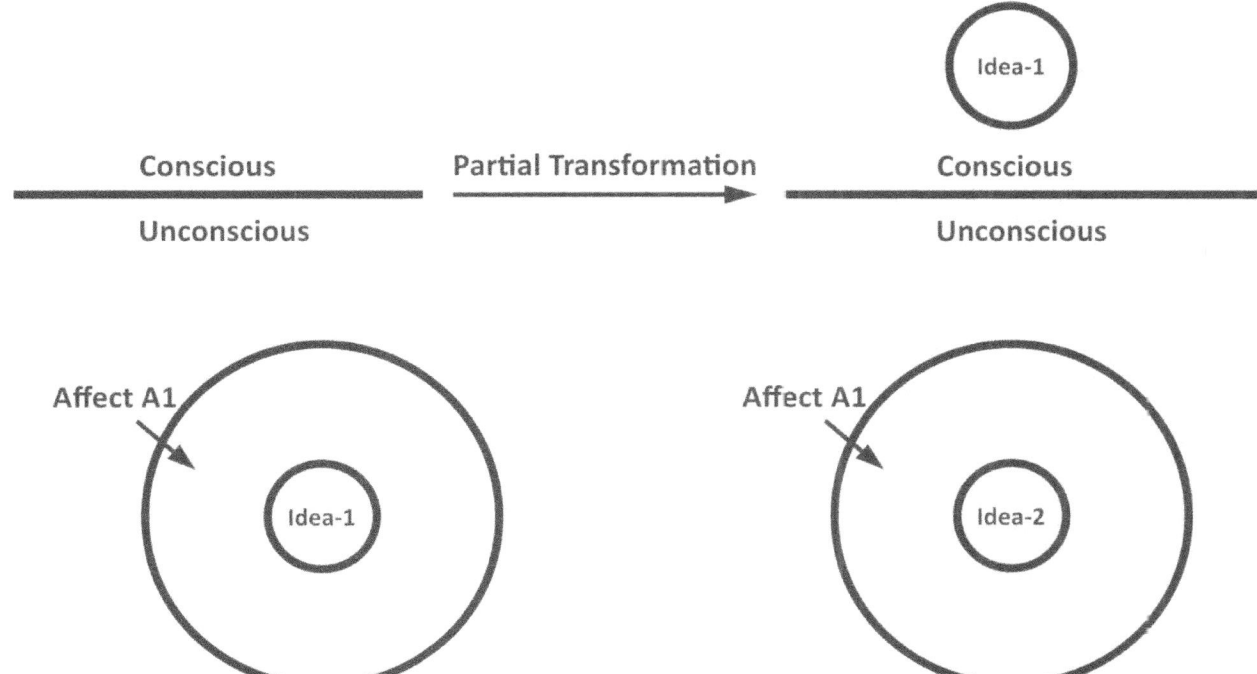

AFFECT RE- ATTACHING TO ANOTHER IDEA

6. **What is the general model of the mind which most schools follow?**

   Every school of Psychoanalysis has its own understanding of the mind and its own explicit or implicit model of the mind. However for all of Psychoanalysis the general accepted framework of the mind is as given here,

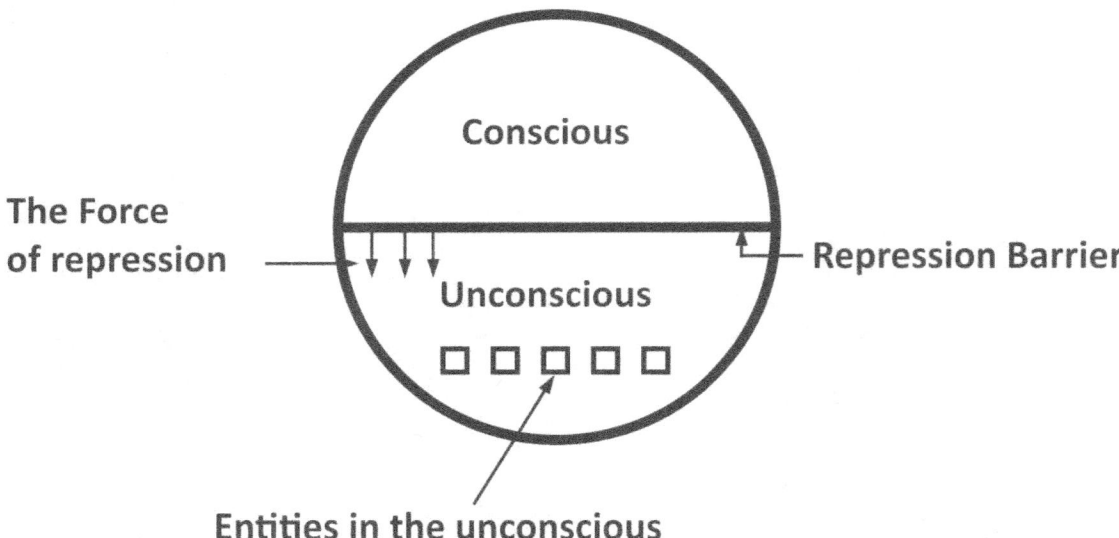

Entities in the unconscious

THE GENERAL MODEL OF MIND IN PSYCHOANALYSIS

The part of mind we are aware of is our conscious mind, the part of our mind we are not aware of is our unconscious mind and the barrier separating the two is the repression barrier. The repression barrier doesn't allow the contents of the unconscious mind to come to the conscious mind. This action of the repression barrier is called 'repression' (and hence it is so named). Complexes responsible for psychopathology are in the unconscious mind.

7. **What is the difference between Psychoanalytic Psychotherapy and Psychodynamic Psychotherapy?**
   Both of them are based on the theory of Psychoanalysis however there are two significant differences between the two approaches. Psychoanalytic Psychotherapy uses 'transference' more than does the psychodynamic Psychotherapy. Psychodynamic Psychotherapy in general is practiced in a relatively more eclectic way compared to Psychoanalytic Psychotherapy. Most Psychodynamic practitioners leverage concepts of more than one school of Psychoanalysis however (puritan) Psychoanalytic practitioners generally tend to follow any one school or approach.

8. **What is Psychoanalytic Psychotherapy like in practice?**
   It is a couch based therapy where the person to be analyzed (analysand) lies down on a comfortable couch which is slightly inclined so that the person is relaxed but doesn't go

to sleep. The room is a quiet slightly lit room to ensure that the person coming for analysis is able to relax, feel secure and be able to go into a reverie like condition where the access to unconscious is easy. The person lies down on the couch and the therapist sits behind him, outside of line of sight of the person (on the couch).

PSYCHOANALYTIC PSYCHOTHERAPY IN PROCESS

The person on the couch speaks whatever comes to his mind without any censure –this is called free association- and the therapist tries to uncover the unconscious contents and templates from what the person is speaking. He brings the same to the notice of the person and this is called giving an 'interpretation' which is the primary job (though not the only job) of the therapist.

9. **Why is the therapy room setting so kept and why is the couch used in Psychoanalytic Psychotherapy?**

Psychoanalytic Psychotherapy is based on the premise of making the 'unconscious complex' conscious. However since the repression barrier doesn't allow material from the unconscious to come to the conscious mind, we do everything we can to weaken the repression barrier. Some of the things we do to facilitate this are,

a) The patient is asked to be on the couch where the couch is slightly elevated at the head part of the patient's body. The idea is that the patient should be relaxed but not fall asleep, he should be in a reverie like condition where the thoughts flow freely without any conscious volition and repression is minimum

b) We ask the patient to speak whatever comes to his mind without any consideration of social norms or logical quality, it is called free association. This helps material slip from the unconscious to the conscious mind

c) The therapist sits behind the head of the patient and so is not visible to the patient which reduces the sense of shame or guilt the patient would have felt while revealing some embarrassing material

d) The sound in the room is kept as low as possible and lighting is also very low to induce a feeling of comfort

e) The amoral and non-judgmental response of the therapist adds to the safety of the patient and after some sessions he is actually able to do free association when the real therapy begins

10. **How long is each session in Psychoanalytic Psychotherapy and how many days a week one has to go for therapy?**
In Psychoanalytic Psychotherapy each session is of 45 or 50 minutes duration. The start and end of the session timings are strictly adhered to. Even if the patient is late, the end of the session still is the same. The patient has to come for 3 to 5 days a week for Psychoanalytic Psychotherapy in most cases. In some cases 1 day per week or 2 day per week is also done but those are rare instances. Classically anything less than 3 days per week is not considered rigorous enough. Psychoanalytic Psychotherapy can go on from a few months to years based on the nature of the problem.

11. **Is there a contract between the patient and the therapist?**
Yes, the contract covers assurance of confidentiality, the therapist can't divulge any information he gets during therapy to anyone without explicit consent of the patient. This therapist also can't use any material he may come across in therapy for research purposes without explicit consent of the patient. The contract also specifies the fee per session and the weekly or monthly or session wise payment terms.

Apart from the legal contract a framework is worked out between the patient and the therapist on the boundaries to be respected during therapy for example if the patient feels angry towards the therapist can he use bad words? This is called setting the boundaries.

The patient and the therapist are supposed to interact only during the session and never outside of the session timings (except under emergency). The two are never supposed to interact in social situations. While the patient is expected to reveal himself completely the therapist is expected to be completely anonymous and reveal nothing about himself to the patient. The therapist is expected to be the blank screen.

12. **Has the efficacy of Psychoanalytic Psychotherapy been researched compared to other psychotherapies?**

Yes it has been done and Psychoanalytic Psychotherapy has proved to be one of the good options for long term therapy. Especially for many of the neurotic diseases for which there is not much in the area of Psychiatry, Psychoanalytic Psychotherapy is surely a good option.

13. **With respect to 'relapse' how does Psychoanalytic Psychotherapy compare with other forms of Psychotherapy?**

Psychoanalytic Psychotherapy performs very well on this front. Relapse is one of the least for problems treated with Psychoanalytic Psychotherapy. It seems natural since this therapy heals at the roots. The counterpoint is that this therapy takes a long time to reach down to the roots of pathology and it calls for great amount of effort and ability on part of both the patient and the therapist.

14. **Does Psychoanalytic Psychotherapy have variants?**

Yes there are many schools of thought within Psychoanalysis like the Freudian School, Jungian School, Kleinien School, Lacanian School and so on. Each school has its variant of therapy however these variations are all within the broad boundaries of Psychoanalytic Psychotherapy.

15. **Which are the schools within Psychoanalysis and in what part of the world is any given school popular?**

There is no country in the world where only one school of Psychoanalysis is exclusively practiced, however some schools are more popular than others. On this basis an indicative list of schools and areas where are popular is given here,

School of Psychoanalysis	Popular where in the world
Sigmund Freud	Asia, Europe, America
Carl Jung	Europe, USA
Lacan	France, South America
Winnicott	UK
ISTDP	USA
Kohut	USA

16. **Can the Psychoanalytic schools be classified in conceptual terms under some broad categories?**

Yes there are many ways of classifying all schools of Psychoanalysis under a few broad categories. One classification is given here,

a) Drive school — Freudian School
b) Object relations school — Kleinien School
c) Ego school — Anna Freud's School
d) Self Psychology school — Kohutian School

17. Can every school of Psychoanalysis heal every pathology with efficacy or is there is school-pathology connect?

Every school of Psychoanalysis has its strengths and weaknesses and so there is a group of pathologies where it is strong and another group where it is weak. Freudian approach is very strong in case of oedipal pathologies, Kleinien in terms of problem rooted in early splitting and object relations, Kohutian in defective self formation. Each school has its areas of strength and weaknesses and hence each school is strong or weak in dealing with a set of given pathologies. However no school will officially acknowledge it.

18. Is it true that Psychoanalytic Psychotherapy takes us back to childhood to heal most of our psychological problems?

Yes it is true, most of our problems are rooted in our childhood and so Psychoanalytic Psychotherapy takes us there to help us heal the problem at its roots and forever

19. Is it true that in the process of Psychoanalytic Psychotherapy the patient often develops intense love or intense hate for the therapist?

Yes it is true. It happens because the hidden feelings the patient has in real life towards some emotionally significant people are thrown on the therapist. The task of therapy is to work through these emotions by creating distance, understanding and insight.

20. Is there a way Psychoanalytic Psychotherapy can be made shorter and intense?

Yes, one school that has now come up is called ISTDP (Intensive Short Term Dynamic Psychotherapy) founded by Dr. Habib Devanloo. This therapy takes the best of Psychoanalytic Psychotherapy and CBT and tries to create a short term intense therapy. The therapy has shown great efficacy in healing and with a very low rate of relapse. However this therapy needs a good ego strength and a motivated co-operation on the part of the patient.

21. Who comes for Psychoanalysis and why?

Patients (or analysands or as say would say clients) come through three routes,

a) Where a Psychiatrist refers them for therapy in addition to his drugs.
b) Patients who know about Psychotherapy and wish to heal themselves with it. Many of them also come inorder to avoid a Psychiatrist.
c) Those who don't have a pathology but are guided by the Socratian desire to know themselves

22. What type of patients are best suited for Psychoanalytic Psychotherapy?

Patients who are educated, motivated to undergo therapy, ready to be open about themselves, with an ability to articulate ones thoughts and feelings, ready for accepting new insights, accepting of a long term therapy and not completely psychotic. These are the features of a classical 'fit' patient for Psychoanalysis.

23. How does Psychoanalysis stand in the light of current neurological research?

Neurological research can only investigate a few of concepts and claims of Psychoanalysis and that too not in great depth. Investigating complex issues like projection, projective identification, reaction formation, splitting are far off the radar. Yet whatever little (research) has become possible has on the whole been positive for Psychoanalysis. It is more likely that future neurological research will strengthen rather than demolish the basic concepts and approach of Psychoanalysis (not necessary all schools will fare equally).

24. Why does Psychoanalytic Psychotherapy take so long?

Generally because of two reasons, one it deals with problems that are rooted very deep in the psyche and two because all of us have resistance to feeling intense feelings of guilt, shame, fear, anger etc. and so we avoid seeing or acknowledging presence of such material in our minds which can trigger these (avoided) emotions. The combined effect of the two leads to Psychoanalysis taking so long.

25. Is it equally efficacious in all countries or does it depend on culture?

In theory Psychoanalysis is a theory of the human mind and so has to be universally applicable. However in practice there are cultures where guided and prescriptive therapies (like CBT or RET or Logo therapy) work better than free, insight driven and self responsibility oriented theories (like Psychoanalysis). Also in many cultures it is difficult for people to be honest about themselves especially involving issues like sexuality, aggression, shame and guilt and in these cultures perhaps other therapies may be more suited. However in every country there is a group of people who stand to benefit immensely from Psychoanalysis.

26. Can Psychoanalytic Psychotherapy be taken along with medications?

Yes and infact in a majority of cases the patients in therapy are also on psychiatric medication. In serious cases the combined treatment of psychiatric drugs and psychotherapy offers good results.

27. Can Psychoanalytic Psychotherapy be taken along with any other Psychotherapy?

Generally at the same time no. At any given time it is better to be confined to any one therapy and one therapist. There can be conflicts in analysis with regard to analyzing any problem between schools of therapies or between analysts leading to confusion and confrontation. So, one at a time please.

28. What are the benefits of Psychoanalytic Psychotherapy?

Enhanced self awareness, knowing the way one's unconscious works, our hidden desires and fears and defenses we deploy in everyday living. It also enables us to know others better by knowing better their ways of behavior and defenses. It also allows us to better make choices about ourselves and live more authentically. Lastly ofcourse we go to therapy for healing something in ourselves and there ofcourse we benefit less or more.

29. Does gender of the patient and the therapist make a difference to therapy?

In theory the position is that gender doesn't make much of a difference in the long run however in the initial part of therapy it may be that if both are of the same gender it is easier to open up and feel less embarrassed about especially sexual issues. Similarly, in terms of transference it is easier to have it stronger and quickly on the therapist of the opposite gender. In the long run however, it doesn't make much difference and all the issues come up in therapy regardless of the gender of the patient or the therapist. Culturally in many countries women often prefer going (or are forced to go) to women therapists, which is more of a social phenomenon than having to do with efficacy of therapy being linked to the gender.

30. Is Psychoanalytic Psychotherapy costly?

Yes compared to other therapies Psychoanalytic Psychotherapy is generally a costly option. The cost per session in USA can range from $50 to $500 while in developing countries like India the cost per session range from $10 to $100. In the spirit of global outsourcing lot of therapy is now shifting to Skype where therapists from developing countries are providing affordable services to patients in developed countries.

31. Why is it so costly and not easily available across the world?

Psychoanalysis is costly owing to two reasons. One, because it aspires to go deep and so it needs many sessions, spread over a long period of time. Secondly in many countries like for instance in USA, the cost and time involved in becoming a psychoanalyst is too high which leads to two things, one there are few gooc analysts and second that they charge their sessions too high.

32. What is the generic sequential flow of events in Psychoanalytic Psychotherapy?

Exceptions apart, the generic sequential flow of event is depicted here,

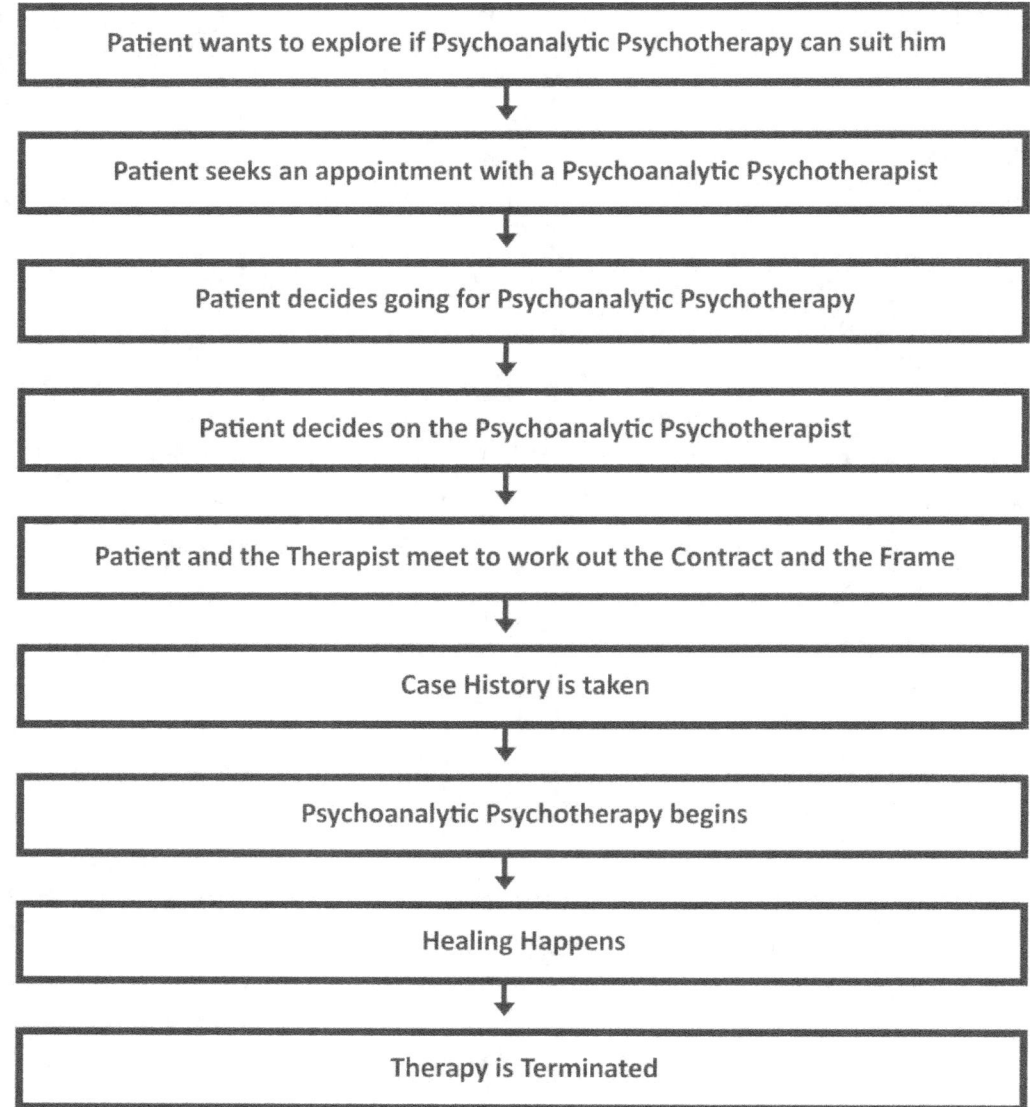

THE SEQUENTIAL PROCESS OF PSYCHOANALYTIC PSYCHOTHERAPY

33. What is 'Technique' in Psychoanalysis?

Psychoanalysis can be divided into the 'conceptual part' and the 'technique part'. Technique refers to many things including,

a) The setting of the frame (which includes, no. of sessions per week, fees, venue, timing etc.) within which both the therapist and the patient will meet each other

b) Whether the therapy will be face to face, on the couch or can start with face to face and then move on to the couch

c) Whether it is going to be a psychodynamic Psychotherapy (which is less dependent on transference analysis and more eclectic) or is it going to strictly be Psychoanalytic

d) During the course of therapy when to give interpretation and when to give support or holding to the patient

e) Issues related to transference, counter-transference, projective identification, holding and others (which shall be done in later part of the book) also are important parts of technique

34. What is the frame in Psychoanalysis?

Frame is referred to the framework within which therapy happens and the therapist and the patient meet and interact with each other. Frame includes the following issues,

a) The no. of sessions per week

b) The day and timing of the sessions

c) The beginning and end of the session at exact timings

d) The interaction between the therapist and the patient being confined only to the therapy room and not outside unless there is an emergency or there is a legally binding necessity

e) First that the patient is free to speak not to act out. Second that there can be limits on how far the patient can go in using bad language while in anger against the therapist

f) That there will no relationship between the patient and the therapist except that being a therapeutic relationship

g) No benefit in cash or kind can be given by the patient (except the fees) to the therapist or vice-versa

In many countries the therapist and the patient have to sign a contract as they enter into therapy and the contract often details out the above and other legal aspects.

35. What is a case history?

The process of therapy begins with taking a case history. The case history includes all the details of the patient including his personal particulars, medical history, psychological history, family history, the history of his problems and their development over time and his views on self, life and the world.

At the end of the case history the therapist arrives at a tentative Psychoanalytic understanding of the patient's problems and an understanding of how his problems would have probably developed over time and hence how to proceed in therapy.

Ofcourse the tentative formulation gets refined as one goes deep into therapy.

36. What is free association?

The patient as he is asked to be on the couch is expected to speak out whatever comes to his mind in terms of thoughts, feelings, visuals, sound or any sensation in the body. The mind is not given any objective, any moral norm to follow and without any censorship anything that comes up in the mind is allowed to come up and the same is expressed, this free expression is called free association.

37. What is an interpretation?

The patient as he is making free association, the therapist offers interpretation which brings to light to the patient the unconscious motivation or unconscious defense involved in his free association. The insight so created by an interpretation brings about transformation, healing, self awareness, a knowledge of how his unconscious mind is working, how the pathology is at work and hence what needs to be done for healing.

When an interpretation is offered, it may be right or half right or wrong. If it is right, the patient feels a movement in him as an insight happens and starts operating. It is the key fitting and opening a lock. It is a distinctly moving and involving experience mostly resulting in a positive change.

38. What is a process note?

After every session the therapist is supposed to write down verbatim exactly what he and the patient said during the session and how he felt during the session and what were the gains or otherwise in his view. Some therapists don't write down for every session but only for those sessions they feel were eventful. Many therapists only write down the verbatim record of what the patient and the therapist said and not their own feelings or opinions. Process notes are discussed often by the therapist with a senior therapist called the Supervisor, always with the permission of the patient

39. What is supervision?

Since no therapist is perfect and he has his own psychological baggage, supervision is a tool designed to ensure that the therapist doesn't reduce the efficacy of the therapy owing to his personal short comings and also that the efficacy is enhanced and enriched with a neutral and experienced opinion.

Every therapist is supposed to have a supervisor who is generally a more senior analyst. The therapist with the consent of the patient shares process notes with the supervisor and they discuss how best to enhance the efficacy of therapy. Even while sharing the process note with the supervisor, the name and identity of the patient is kept confidential. The supervisor never comes to know the identity of the patient.

40. Can Psychoanalytic sessions be video or audio recorded?
No they can't be recorded owing to two reasons, First is confidentiality (and fear it creates in the patient) and second is the issue that the presence of the recording device creates a third presence in the room and distorts the two person situation of therapy.

However the new technique of ISTDP (Intensive short term dynamic Psychotherapy) which is based on Psychoanalytic theory does video record every session and the session can be seen individually both by the patient and the therapist to see where something right or less right happened and how to go forward.

41. How does Psychoanalysis actually work?
It is a difficult question but it is believed it works in the following ways,

a) Any therapy one takes has some generic benefits like being able to speak out and empty one's heart without a fear of criticism or judgment, being able to spare time thinking about ones problems on a regular systematic basis and get right interpretation or explanation from a trained person. These generic benefits like all therapies are available in Psychoanalysis also and this partly contributes to healing

b) By revisiting and reliving the difficult past events, the unconscious events become conscious and the blocked feelings are released and that partly leads to healing

c) Objective realistic analysis of oneself allows one to be realistic and accept reality as it is and that partly leads to healing

d) In an unconscious way the patient absorbs the peace, the amoral non judgmental environment and hears himself speak aloud his inner most feelings, this into itself leads partly to healing

e) The patient also absorbs unconsciously the goodness of the therapist as a stable non-judgmental empathic object and this too partly leads to healing

For each person how much each of the above leads to healing is different.

42. Can a therapist enter into a relationship with a patient?

No ethically the therapist can't have a relationship with the patient even if the patient request's so, while the therapy is on and for two years after the termination of therapy. Morally the therapist also should not get into a relationship with any person close to the patient.

43. What is a cancellation policy?

In Psychoanalytic Psychotherapy, the patient has to pay if he doesn't come to the session without informing it prior in advance. How much prior in advance he has to inform, is covered by cancellation policy. Every analyst has his way of working and his cancellation policy. For example a one week cancellation policy would mean that if the patient informs one week in advance for his not coming to a session then he is not charged for that session however if he informs two or three days in advance then he has to pay for the session even if he doesn't come for the session. When the analyst is sick or on a vacation then ofcourse the patient doesn't have to pay.

This is so designed because in therapy as one goes near the root of the problem the patient has to face intense feelings of anxiety, pain, guilt, shame, envy etc. and many times inorder to avoid it patients skip sessions at that very stage of analysis when maximum gains and healing is possible. If the patient has to pay for the missed sessions then this tendency to avoid difficult emotions and thereby healing is reduced and so the importance of paying for missed sessions.

Patients generally find paying for missed sessions very disturbing and they often bring it up in therapy. In addition to bringing out many unconscious issues, the collateral benefit often is of learning reality adjustment where everything we want can't be as we wish and we have to adjust to things we don't like.

44. What is termination?

Termination refers to closing of therapy after its objectives have been achieved or the patient is empowered for reality adjustment. Generally it takes about one to two weeks for closing the therapy revisiting the entire journey, learning from it and ensuring consolidation of gains of therapy.

45. **Can a therapist suggest that the therapy with him be terminated and that the patient should seek help with some other therapist?**

This is an extremely rare case but I have seen it happen where a therapist after knowing the patient felt he was not adequately equipped to handle the patient and provide him the necessary healing experience. He referred the patient to someone else after talking to the patient and the next therapist.

It can also happen if the therapist decides to shift location or stop practicing as a psychotherapist or takes on some assignment other than therapy and has no time to provide therapy, he may request for a termination of therapy.

Exceptionally if the patient becomes too violent or manipulative or resistant or no results are forthcoming then too a termination from the side of the therapist can be suggested. At times if the therapist becomes too old or sick to continue therapy or if the patient gets into a financial difficulty and can't pay the therapist then too a termination of therapy may be suggested by the therapist.

46. **How does research happen in Psychoanalysis?**

Research happens by analysis of patients and self analysis by Psychoanalysts. Patient research can happen only with the explicit consent of the patient and not otherwise. The nature of confidential and subjective data we are dealing with makes it difficult for Psychoanalysis to mimic the type of research done in physical sciences, life sciences or other social sciences.

47. **Is hypnosis used in Psychoanalytic Psychotherapy?**

No it is not. Sigmund Freud in very early days of Psychoanalysis found two problems with using hypnosis, one was that everyone can't be put in hypnosis and second that suggestions given in hypnosis don't always work out and many work only for a short time. This led him to leave hypnosis and create the technique of free association which is used in Psychoanalysis.

48. **Is there any code of conduct for Psychoanalytic Psychotherapists?**

Yes there is an ethical code of conduct. There are guidelines laid out by the IPS (International Psychoanalytic Society). For example the therapist and the patient can't enter into a relationship not only during the conduct of therapy but for two years even after the completion of therapy. Similarly the therapist is bound by the code of ethics to maintain the confidentiality (except under emergency or when ordered by law) related to any material he comes across in the therapy process.

49. Who is fit to be a psychotherapist?

To be a good therapist one has to have an enduring interest in the working of the human mind and people. One has to be interested in relating to people and helping them to heal and realize their potential. One also needs to have a gift of articulation, creativity, empathy and an ability to keep confidentiality.

Lastly this is not a mono skill job, one needs an exposure to philosophy, history and a wide real life experience of varied types of people and varied types of experiences which one can creatively use, inorder to be a good therapist apart from ofcourse the conceptual knowledge and therapy practice. An eclectic openness to other schools and modalities of alternative healing becomes a great asset to the therapist.

50. Is a master's in psychology or clinical psychology enough to practice as a Psychoanalyst?

No it is not. At the minimum (and this may differ across countries) you have to undergo a minimum 3 year programme that involves conceptual learning, your own analysis for atleast 2 years, seeing atleast two patients under supervision for 2 years and doing a thesis or two papers, to be a psychoanalyst. So in no way, a simple general post-graduation in Clinical Psychology can empower you to be a psychoanalyst.

51. How can I become a Psychoanalyst?

Different countries have different requirements to enroll in the Psychoanalytic programme. Some countries require a degree in Psychology, some other countries require a degree in Medicine. In India (and many other countries) you only need a graduation in any area to enroll in the programme. However you have to enroll in a university department or a Psychoanalytic training centre which has been recognized by the IPS (International Psychoanalytic Society). In case your Institute or center is not recognized by IPA then you have to earn a official master's degree or an equivalent certificate or award.

52. Why does it take so long to become a psychoanalyst?

There are two sets of reasons for this. One has to do with the regulatory framework which in certain countries like in USA makes it difficult at the entry itself. In USA you have to be a MD psychiatrist or a PhD in Clinical Psychology or a PhD in Social Work to enroll for Psychoanalysis and then you have to undergo 3-7 years of your own analysis along with ofcourse the conceptual learning, see patients under supervision and write atleast two papers based on your work. This takes a lot of time. Secondly there is an aspect of eligibility criteria from International Psychoanalytic association which demands long analysis and writing papers on one's work under supervision.

Apart from the above two sets of reasons, often the training analysis every candidate has to undergo during the training goes much longer than anticipated (often owing to pathology of the trainee) and this compounds the time problem.

53. In India where are the various schools of Psychoanalysis anchored?

In India the Freudian school is anchored at Kolkota, Ahmedabad and Delhi, the Kleinien school is anchored at Mumbai, the Jungian school at Bangalore and the Winnicottian school at Delhi.

54. Can violent patients be treated with Psychoanalytic Psychotherapy?

The potentially violent patients have to be calmed down with psychiatric drugs before therapy can happen. Since the therapist is alone with the patient, chances are not taken and if the aggression is on-going, therapy sessions are stopped till the patient has calmed down. Even after medication is given in such cases, in asylums or psychiatric departments, strong security personnel are kept ready outside the therapy room, available at a bell call, in case the need be for protecting the therapist.

55. Is Psychoanalytic Psychotherapy done the same way across age groups? How do you do therapy for children?

Children can't articulate their feelings and thoughts as adults do and also their healing can't be as insight based as it is for adults. Thus for children instead of couch based therapy, play therapy is used. Children are given toys or games to play and the therapist observes the unconscious as it comes out in play and games. For example if the child is angry with parents, if he is given a set of family dolls and other articles, he may break the neck of the mother toy or the father toy or throw it away. Children can also be asked to complete a half complete story, draw a picture or complete a picture, speak any word that comes to their mind and so on. The process is different but underlying understanding continues to be Psychoanalytic.

56. Does Psychoanalysis believe in God?

Except for Jung no important Psychoanalyst has written to express his belief or respect or need for God. Traditional Psychoanalysis sees in the concept of 'God' a need for a protective all providing omnipotent father or mother figure which we as infants wanted and the desire continues in us even as we become adults. This is essentially an infantile desire and not rooted in reality. Psychoanalysis (except in Jungian approach) wants you to overcome the anxiety of living in a world without God and engage with reality without the crutches of concepts of immortality, rebirth or God. In that philosophical sense it is a very secular, non-believing existential approach to living.

57. Is Psychoanalytic Psychotherapy dependent on one's religious beliefs?

Religious beliefs don't generally affect Psychoanalytic Psychotherapy, however if some one's religious beliefs are so strong that he is not able to accept truths about himself or others than a problem comes up. People with such strong beliefs may eject out of therapy and discontinue it or else they may start with many sessions of confrontation and very slowly over a long period of time, be ready for insights.

58. In which academic areas today Psychoanalysis is being used apart for the purpose of Psychotherapy?

Psychoanalysis is a science of human mind and so it aspires to the status of a mother science in the area of reality that comes into being owing to the working of the human mind. Thus all of humanities and social sciences are areas where Psychoanalysis can be used. Some of the areas to mention are,

a) Economics – to understand behavioral economics and stock market behavior
b) Marketing – to understand consumer behavior in aspects of product management, brand management and retailing
c) Film studies – to understand how people understand movies and how they respond to movies by liking or not liking it
d) History – to understand behavior of important personalities at critical times in human history. Psychoanalysis of historical figures is of great interest to many. Not to forget how and why people thought and behaved the way they did at given times in history
e) Arts and Literature – to understand the creator's unconscious mind of which the art or piece of literature is a product. Also to understand how as an independent entity (text) the work of art or literature takes meaning in the mind of the audience

59. On what grounds is Psychoanalysis criticized?

Psychoanalysis has its own share of criticism and it is criticized by critics on many grounds some of which are,

a) It is not scientific enough in the sense it deals with subjective data in a very subjective way and the kind of evidence and assessment which is done in other social sciences is not done here. There is also no fixed structure, predictability of results of a given measure or a time based outcome expectation and hence it is not something rigorous enough to be called a science.

b) There is a feminist critic which says, it is a man's science and that it doesn't understand women nor there is an empathic standpoint from point of feminine existence and that the responsibility of pathology in many of the schools is unequally and irrationally put on women, the mother. Also there is no appreciation or attempt at improvement of the feminine existence and the way it is annexed by a patriarchal culture

c) The conservative critic is that it is too much of individualism and almost a licentious approach to morality and what it denounces as repression is the very reason why civilization stands today. The amoral, agnostic and individualistic stand of Psychoanalysis is something severely criticized by the conservative and religious groups

d) There is a criticism from pragmatists that Psychoanalysis dramatizes ordinary issues and it is more of an artistic rather than a pragmatic enterprise and that infact no one can live by its principles not even the therapists

e) From outside of Psychoanalysis but within psychology there is a criticism that Psychoanalysis over emphasis the unconscious aspect of the psyche and the primacy of childhood. There is also a criticism of giving out of proportion significance to sexuality and aggression and less than deserved significance to positive aspects of living and the search for meaning in life

f) From within Psychoanalysis there has been criticism of one school by another. Some of it pertains to the misplaced claims on universality of certain concepts like the Oedipus complex. Other inter-school criticisms pertain to significance of various concepts in the causation of any given psycho-pathology

g) Karl Popper used to call Psychoanalysis a pseudo-science since it does not full fil the criteria of a rigorous science because it does not pass the test of falsifiability i.e. when a claim is made that x causes y one should not only be able to prove that x causes y but also that y is not caused by anything else (say z). One wonders how many of the sciences we have can pass that test.

60. Does Psychoanalysis have a future?

Certainly yes. Psychoanalysis is a very powerful theory of the internal world and is one of the most promising efforts ever made to understand the mysteries of the human mind. As neurology progresses and more scientific evaluation becomes possible, much of Psychoanalysis will stand validated and the rest refined. The future regardless of the present 'pharmacological inclination' is bright and Psychoanalysis will not be enhance understanding and healing in the area of mental health but will also enrich Homeopathy and a great number of areas in Humanities.

Psychoanalysis is in essence, a cure through love - Sigmund Freud

Sigmund Freud

the words of truth are always paradoxical - Lao Tzu

1. **Who was Sigmund Freud?**

   Dr Sigmund Freud (DOB 6-5-1856) was trained first as a doctor (neurologist). He lived in Austria, Vienna till World War II and after that at London. He is the founding father of Psychoanalysis.

2. **What is Freud's contribution to the area of Psychoanalysis?**

   Dr Sigmund Freud founded and established Psychoanalysis. He discovered the existence of the unconscious mind. He developed a model of the mind, discovered the psycho-sexual stages of developments, created the treatment model of Psychoanalytic Psychotherapy, published studies on 'interpretation of dreams' and wrote extensively on many other areas.

3. **How did Freud start creating his theories?**

   Freud started with cases of hysteria and he found that when he talked with the patients about their emotional life and problems the patients reported relief. The more he talked and the more it resolved emotional issues of patients the more they reported some relief, this was laughingly then called 'the talking cure'. Freud however persisted and found that when deep seated childhood emotional conflicts were resolved, healing happened. Freud from here started analyzing psychologically the patients and their dreams to create the first principles of Psychoanalysis to which he later added principles and concepts, he found from his own self-analysis.

4. **What is the unconscious mind?**

   It was believed before Sigmund Freud that the mind is what we are aware of. However Sigmund Freud discovered that the mind consists of two parts the part we are aware of, the conscious mind and the part we are not aware of, the unconscious mind. The idea is that outside of our awareness also there is a part of the mind that works independently. Our entire mind is not in our control or awareness. The unconscious mind is very active and is responsible for most of our psychological problems (pathology or psycho-pathology).

5. **Why does the unconscious mind exist?**

The unconscious mind exists because of many reasons. First, our ability of conscious processing is limited and so a great part of the stimuli we receive have to be stored away in the unconscious to avoid over flooding of the conscious mind. Second, there is a natural time related erosion in memory and long past memories have to be stored away. Lastly and most importantly from a Psychoanalytic standpoint memories which if made conscious can lead to uncomfortable feelings of anger, fear, pain, guilt, shame or envy have to be kept away from awareness and hence are stored in the unconscious mind. From Psychoanalytic standpoint, the unconscious material of traumatic or potentially traumatic type is of great importance and is believed to be responsible for psycho - pathology.

6. **What is the topographical model of the mind?**

Freud developed a model of the mind to explain how the mind is constituted and how it works. Freud in his life time developed two models of the mind, the first model was called the 'topographical model' of the mind and the second model was called the 'structural model' of the mind.

The topographical model says that the mind consists of three layers, the conscious part (we are aware of), the pre-conscious part (we can be aware of with a little effort) and the unconscious part (we are not aware of nor can we be aware of by will, it needs a lot of effort and often Psychotherapy to make something in the unconscious come to our awareness).

There is a layer between the pre-conscious and the unconscious mind called the repression barrier and this repression barrier represses the contents of the unconscious mind and doesn't allow them to come to the conscious mind. The purpose of this repression is prevent feelings of fear, guilt, shame, envy and other unpleasant feelings from arising which will happen if the contents of the unconscious mind become conscious.

The topographical model of the mind graphically is depicted here,

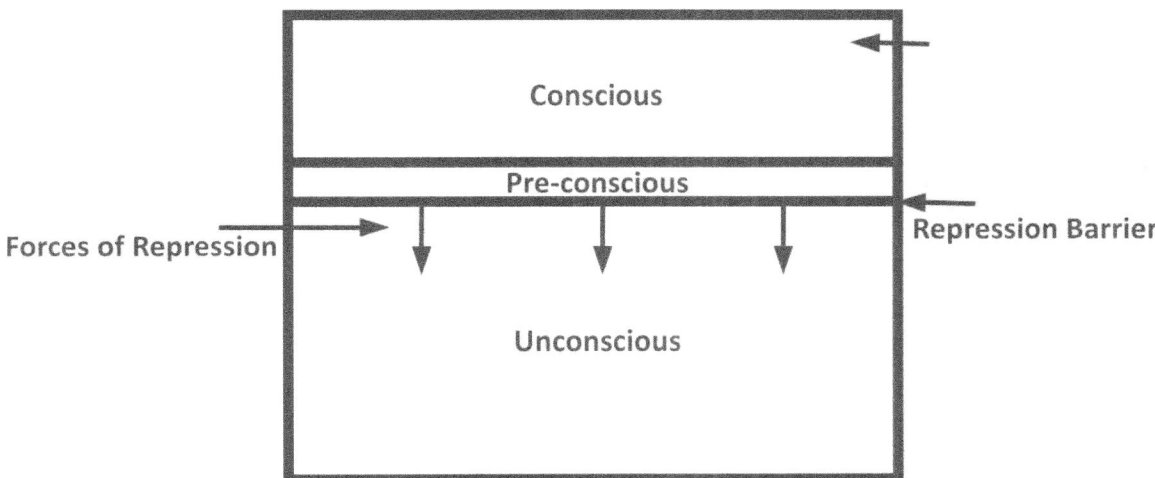

FREUD'S TOPOGRAPHICAL MODEL OF THE MIND

7. What is the structural model of the mind?

The structural model of the mind is the second model of the mind developed by Freud. The structural model was developed a few years after the topographical model of the mind. The structural model states that there are three active parts of the mind that is, The Id, The Ego and The Superego.

Id is the reservoir of instincts. Id has the desire for infinite pleasure and a tendency to release aggression in face of fear or frustration of desire. Id is the most primitive part of man. The Ego is the agent of reality and it tries to modulate the Id inorder to ensure survival and growth of the person. The Ego enables us to modulate the demands of the Id in the face of reality. The Superego is the reservoir of ideals and morals (inhibitions). The Superego has two aspects one which says Thou Shall (the ideals) and the second that says Thou Shall Not (the inhibitions). The Superego thus is almost in a moral sense the opposite of Id. The Ego has to balance the contrasting and competing demands of the Id and the Superego to ensure survival and growth of the individual.

The Id is completely unconscious. The Ego and Superego are both partly conscious and partly unconscious.

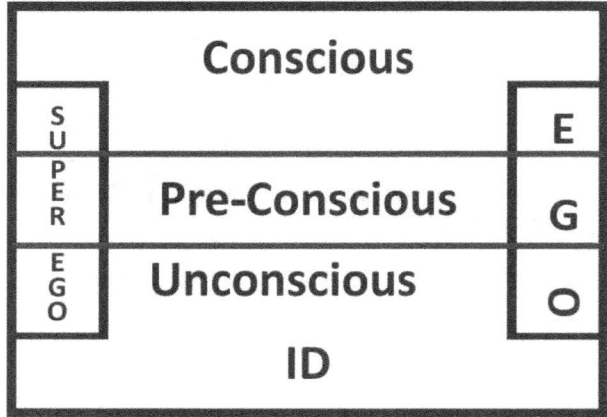

FREUD'S STRUCTURAL MODEL OF THE MIND

8. **What is the Pleasure Principle?**

Freud believed the core guiding principle for the human mind is maximizing of pleasure and minimizing of pain. This principle is called the pleasure principle and it is at the root of all that we do.

9. **What is Libido?**

Freud believed that there is a psychic energy that is active in the human psyche which he called the Libido. When we think deeply or feel intensely, what we are doing is that we are investing the subject of our thought or feeling with this psychic energy. Libido movements and transformations in the psyche are extremely important in Freudian thinking.

10. **What are Psycho-sexual stages of development?**

The psychological development of a human being during childhood passes through distinct phases. In each phase certain processes happen, leading to development of certain aspects of the psyche. Freud discovered that in the age range of 0-5 years (some would say 0-7 years) the child passed through distinct phases of psychological development which he called the psychosexual stages of development. There are three distinct phases of psycho-sexual development,

a) The Oral Phase   (0-2.5 years)
b) The Anal phase   (2.5-3.5 or 4 years)
c) The Phallic phase   (4-5 or 7 years)

(Some experts add a urethral phase to the three phases and make it a four phase model. The Phallic phase is also called the Oedipal phase)

Each stage if passed successfully leads to some specific gains and if in any stage a problem occurs, then some specific psycho-pathology takes root which may man fest immediately or in most cases after puberty. If at any stage a problem occurs, it may or may not affect the next stage of psychic development.

The latency period follows after the phallic phase and lasts till puberty. During the latency period the focus shifts to the body and in most individuals a lid is put on the psychological issues and they are put away. With puberty, the unresolved issues of pre-latency phase again rise up with great intensity and that is how the teen years and especially post puberty years are those where most psycho-pathologies become explicit.

11. What is Oedipus complex?

Freud discovered that between 4-5 years (some will say 4-7 years) of age the child develops a romantic and sexual desire for the parent of the opposite gender and a desire to kill the parent of the same gender. This also leads to the fear that the person of the same gender will know of these desires the child is harboring and so the parent of the same gender will castrate and kill the child. The child at the same time also carries a strong guilt for having such desire and aggression. This set of psychic phenomenon is generally referred to as the Oedipus complex.

12. How can the unconscious be known?

The unconscious is by definition something that the conscious mind doesn't know. However there are some ways of knowing the unconscious and five popular approaches include,

  a. Slips

  Slips happen when some unconscious material is able to 'slip stealthily' through the repression barrier. Slips of tongue, slips in writing, and slips in listening allow us to analyze the unconscious contents and templates which lead to these slips in the first place. Unconscious desires, fears and defenses can be analyzed using the material and nature of slips.

  b. Dreams

While asleep the repression barrier is weak (but not absent) and so material from unconscious comes up as dreams. From analyzing the dreams one can go to the unconscious roots (latent content) of the dream, which is the material in the unconscious consisting of desires, fears and associated defenses.

c. Free association

In therapy the unconscious is understood by understanding the content and feeling aspect of the material derived from free association. The material of free association which consists of expressing whatever comes to the mind be it thoughts, visuals, feelings or anything else, allows us to analyze it and reach to the unconscious roots of it, providing us a knowledge of the unconscious.

d. Hypnosis

Hypnosis is also an approach to know the unconscious by suspending the working of the conscious mind in a trance state and have a direct access to the unconscious.

e. Art

Art is created when the reality orientation (Ego) is temporarily de-emphasized and the creative forces use imagination, memory and the material of the unconscious to create something. Thus be it a painting, music, film or literature, there is a significant amount of involvement of the unconscious in every art. Analyzing the art (creation) one can get knowledge of the unconscious of the artist.

ISTDP (Intensive Short Term Dynamic Psychotherapy founded by Davanloo) tries to access the unconscious by increasing the patient's resistance to a critical level after which the resistance breaks down, providing a radically large and easy access to the unconscious.

13. What is a Defense? What are the types of Defenses?

In Psychoanalysis, the psyche in order to prevent intense feelings of anxiety, pain, guilt, shame, envy and other avoided feelings, undertakes psychic operations to preserve the pleasant homeostasis so far as possible in the psyche. Such psychic operations are called defenses.

Psyche uses many defenses some of which are repression, suppression, displacement, splitting, projection, and projective identification. Three examples are given here,

Repression – This defense is used to repress unpleasant material in the conscious from coming to consciousness. Thus a traumatic childhood beating may be repressed and one may never be able to recall all the details of the event even if one tries hard.

Reaction formation – Someone who feels he is not good looking may exercise a defense of reaction formation and start believing that he is extremely good looking (the opposite of the original feeling or thought)

Displacement – If you are angry with your boss and you take out that angry on house-help, you are using the defense of displacement. You displace anger from one person to another or one object to another.

14. **What is a symptom? What is neurosis and psychosis?**

Symptom –in a strict Psychoanalytic sense- is an attempt at solution of some problem in the unconscious. However it is a dysfunctional solution and so in normal parlance we don't call it a solution at all, rather it is called a problem which has to be solved.

Symptom often tells us what potentially the problem can be in the unconscious and what feelings (affect) are being repressed. The nature of the symptom broadly indicates towards the unconscious problem and a route of therapy.

Neurosis is a state when the patient has psycho-pathology but his connect to reality is intact. He is able to function in the world and also to take care of himself. Innumerable people have neurosis and yet are productive individuals in their organizations. Psychosis is a serious condition where partially or totally the individual loses his connect to reality and starts living in a world of his own. In extreme cases the individual may not be able to take daily care of himself and may also turn violent or get extremely fearful. Psychotic conditions are more difficult to manage and heal than neurotic conditions. 'Neurosis' and 'Psychosis' are words that denote a wide category under which a number of pathologies are covered.

15. **What according to Freud is anxiety?**

Anxiety is explained to be a danger signal which is created to inform the conscious mind that some traumatic material in the unconscious is about to get into awareness and if it so happens, it will create intense feelings related to anger, fear, guilt, shame, envy or something of the type which the individual doesn't wish to experience.

16. How does healing occur according to Freud?

According to Freud and much of Psychoanalysis, it is believed that reason of pathology is that in the unconscious there is a complex (an idea loaded with feelings (affect)). Healing happens when three things happen,

a) The ideational part of the complex comes into the conscious mind and becomes known to the person
b) The affect (feelings) associated with the idea in the unconscious is released
c) The released affect becomes available for wholesome living

17. How does one feel in analysis when a complex is resolved?

It is a very distinct experiential feeling when it happens, and it definitely happens many times, to each person in therapy. One comes to see very vividly an infantile childish logic which was operating for long in one's unconscious. One feels a distinct emotional movement in oneself often accompanied by sensations in the body. One feels a burden long carried is put off the chest.

One feels more alive, more energetic, more positive and more loving and playful. The consolidation of this 'resolution of the complex' as it is called has to be done outside the therapy room to convert gains of therapy into a working reality (in life) and with that an enduring change is instituted in life.

Here we are discussing is something where 'Feeling is Believing'.

18. Can it happen that the idea gets into awareness but the feeling remains in the unconscious?

Yes it is possible and it is not very uncommon. In such a case one feels a minor relief however it doesn't result in fundamental healing. Often in such a case the striving then is to bring out the feeling which is in the unconscious.

In some cases this feeling part (affect) which remains in the unconscious gets associated with some other idea in the unconscious and often creates a new symptom. It is like someone who has a phobia of water now starts having a phobia of animals.

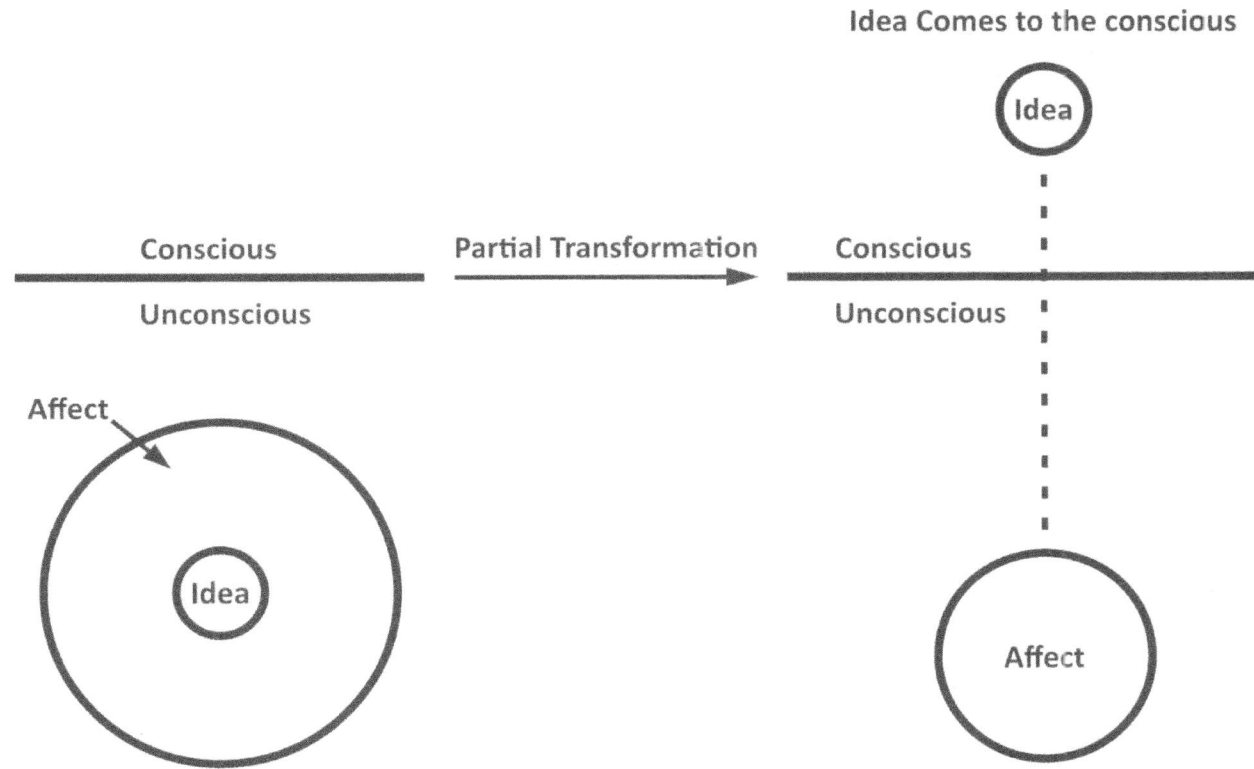

ONLY IDEA BECOMES CONSCIOUS

19. What is Regression?

The psyche in the journey of life when it encounters something very frustrating, fearful or painful which it can't endure, it (the psyche) goes back in time (to some era of childhood) to that era when adequate pleasure and security was available. This going back is called regression. Ofcourse this going back is strictly psychological and not biological.

Take an example. If a man loses in business and there is no hope and life is full of too many challenges, fear and pain, the person may break down. He may start behaving as he used to behave as a child. This is because his psyche in the face of present frustration has gone back to a time when he was happy. His body remains as per his present age (bones can't contract, regression is strictly a psychological phenomenon) however the mind starts operating as if it had gone back in time. This going back is temporary and in most cases the person comes back and is able to lead a normal life after therapy or after the difficulties of life either go away or have been overcome.

Strangely nature has allowed for psychological regression but not for biological regression.

20. What is Transference and Counter Transference?

Freud found that most of his female patients in therapy used to fall in love with him. Fortunately he was very clear that there was nothing in him such that so many women would fall in love with him. This led him to discover that patients transfer on the therapist, feelings they have towards other important people in their lives. This transfer of feelings is called transference. In response to transference the therapist develops a response towards the patient and that is called counter transference. For example the patients love towards the patient can make the therapist anxious or angry (or both).

Both transference and counter transference are unconscious processes and it all happens without any voluntary action. The therapist has to be trained to clearly identify transference and counter-transference so he can distance from both and bring to the notice of the patient the transference that is happening, leading to insight and healing (and at the same time make sure his own counter transference doesn't harm the therapy). Often transference (when it is subtle) is identified by many skilled analysts by recognizing their counter transference.

21. Why are Dreams so important for Psychoanalysis?

Dreams are very important in Psychoanalysis because during sleep our repression barrier (which stops material from the unconscious mind trying to come into the conscious mind) becomes weak and so the hidden material (modified ofcourse) from the unconscious comes out in the form of dreams. The analysis of dreams therefore helps the therapist to understand what is hidden in the unconscious and once that is known, healing becomes easier and faster.

22. What is Dream work?

Even though the repression barrier is weak in dreams it doesn't allow material from the unconscious to go into dreams unless it is modified. The modification has to be 'adequate' (and that is why most dreams appear strange and we are not able to make out any meaning out of it easily) such that the dreamer is not able to make out the real meaning of the dream (the real meaning is in the unconscious). This work of modification done on the contents of the unconscious before allowing it to go into dreams is what is called 'dream work'.

Take an example. An engineering student reported this dream. He was studying in an engineering college in the second year. Marks for one of the subjects (exams for which were held a month back) were put up on the notice board. The student went to see his marks and found he had fourth highest when infact he was expecting the highest and he also found that one of his good friends had got the highest.

That night he had the following dream.

He saw there was a 100 meters Olympic race. As the race began, after some time all runners were left behind by two leading runners who were competing for the first prize. One of the two was a white runner and the second was a black runner. It was stiff competition but in the end the white runner won the race.

What has happened here is that the student wanted highest marks but his friend got it instead. Hence as he was seeing his marks, in the unconscious mind of the student there was envy for his friend and a desire that he should have got the highest marks. However this 'desire' and 'envy' were unacceptable to his 'morality' and hence both were repressed in his unconscious and he never knew he had such feelings.

The feelings of 'unfulfilled desire', 'envy' and 'anger' felt during the day time (unconsciously ofcourse) towards the friend come out in the dream. In the dream he identifies himself with the white runner, his friend with the black runner and defeats him in the dream which in real life could not. The dream thus becomes a means to wish fulfillment. Also the friend being shown as a black man (to humiliate, degrade him and have revenge) and not as good looking as the student brings out the envy and anger the student feels towards his friend.

Why the student had to dream all this and not be able to process it straight during the waking state? It is because his morality would not allow him to be so envious, aggressive and without a sense of fairness for his friend. Thus he (the dreamer) is infact a good (how good can a man be?) friend with strong morality but like everyone else has no control on his unconscious mind.

Here the conversion of the student into the white runner, of his friend into the black runner and other elements of the dream are all done inorder to keep secret the real meaning of the dream so that feelings of guilt don't arise in the dreamer. This makes the dream strange and one struggles to find why such a dream had come to an engineering student who has nothing to do with Olympics. This working upon the real truth in the unconscious and converting it into a strange dream is called Dream Work. The real content in the unconscious is called the 'latent dream content' and the dream as it is actually seen is called the 'manifest dream content'. Dream work converts the latent dream content into manifest dream content.

23. What is Interpretation of Dreams?

Dreams as we see them are mostly strange. The Dream as we see it is called 'manifest dream content'. This is actually a modified version of something that exists in the unconscious called the 'latent dream content' (as we have seen in the last question). Dream Interpretation is the process of undoing the dream work so that from the 'manifest dream content' we reach to the real 'latent dream content' (which is in the unconscious).

24. What is Narcissism?

Narcissism is pathology of being in love with oneself and not being related in a realistic sense to anyone else. It flows from the Greek myth of Narcissus. Freud defined two types in 'Narcissism', the 'primary narcissism' and the 'secondary narcissism'.

Freud believed that in the first few weeks after birth the infant doesn't recognize or relate to others and is completely self contended. This is the state of what he called primary narcissism.

However the infant after some time tries to relate to the mother or parents or care takers. If in the process the infant doesn't get right responses from those he tries to relate to, his attempt of trying to relate and love is frustrated and the infant then decides (ofcourse some infants do it, not all) not to relate to anyone else. He develops a template, 'relating brings pain' and so he goes back to the state of being only with oneself as he was in the first few weeks. This deciding (unconsciously) not to relate to others but only to oneself (ofcourse it is continuum and we are not referring to an absolute relating or not relating) leads to the infant forming very few relationships and that too with people who he feels are either like him or those he can control. This state or orientation is called as secondary narcissism.

25. What is the Freudian understanding about Obsessions and Compulsions?

Obsessions relate to obsessive uncontrollable thoughts or feelings and Compulsions relate to uncontrollable actions one undertakes. Generally obsessions lead to compulsions. It can be checking locks again and again or counting till a particular number before doing anything or washing hands 10 times a day or anything else.

Freudian explanation here is based on the Oedipus complex. The person who has a strong Oedipus complex relieves his guilt and anxiety through the obsessions and compulsions. It involves desire to satisfy the Oedipal desire, guilt related to satisfaction of the Oedipal desire, the anxiety of castration and anxiety of social consequences. It is primarily the anxiety that finds an obsessive and compulsive route to discharge itself while other affects (feelings) often contribute to the qualitative aspect of the obsession or the compulsion. Thus resolving the Oedipus complex is the road to healing in Freudian approach.

Other schools of Psychoanalysis have their own understanding and road to healing.

26. How do we explain bisexuality or homosexuality based on the Oedipus complex?

Freud believed all human beings had both masculinity and femininity in them leading to a potentially bisexual orientation (in conceptual terms not in living practice). Thus every human being would have an Oedipus complex related to the parent of the opposite gender based on heterosexual attraction and an Electra complex (also called the negative Oedipus complex) related to the parent of the same gender based on homosexual attraction.

In heterosexual personalities the Oedipus complex would be strong and Electra complex very weak whereas in homosexual personalities the Electra complex would be strong and the Oedipus complex would be weak whereas in bisexual personalities both Oedipus and Electra complexes would be comparable in strength to each other (not exactly equal in strength although in rare cases it can be so)

27. What does Freud say in his paper Civilization and its Discontents?

The broad argument is that repression to some extent is inevitable if civilization is to exist and also that this repression if carried to its extreme can lead to psycho-pathology. Thus frustration and in some individuals psycho-pathology is a price of civilization. The idea is to be in the 'safe zone' on the continuum of 'asceticism to perversion'. The civilization thus is based on a foundation of repression, frustration and discontent. However yet, it is worthy to be preserved and cherished because it brings in order, love, pleasure and progress far more than it is possible in its absence.

28. What is the central idea in Freud's paper 'Beyond the Pleasure Principle?

Freud was greatly affected both personally and conceptually by the events of World War II. He could see in the war the madness in mankind. He saw how much aggression and sadism human beings have or are capable of. The inability of human beings to control their thirst for power, destructive tendencies and negativity was also for all to see. There was no way the second world war could be explained as being motivated by a search for pleasure which was till then understood as the prime motivation of human behavior.

Also when Freud was treating soldiers returning with a 'war trauma' he found many of them kept repeating (speaking and feeling about) the trauma again and again. At first he felt it was an attempt to slowly master the trauma by taking up small bit of it for processing every time. However he realize over time that it was not only an attempt at mastery and healing but that infact many people like to voluntary go into and savor pain. Pain is relished by many, not only by obvious masochists who hurt themselves and ask others to hurt them and get pleasure out of it but even by many ordinary looking people. Thus the tendency in people to relish pain in some cases consciously and in some people unconsciously came out.

This lead him to revision of his basic premise that the prime objective of human psyche is pleasure maximization and this led him to write a paper 'beyond the pleasure principle' where he talks of relishing of pain by human beings and this path of theorizing takes one aspects of human psyche other than pleasure which are, relishing pain (masochism), self destruction, negativity, destruction of the other (sadism), resistance to all progress and a movement into inertia.

29. What is the Death Instinct?

Towards the end of his life, Freud came to believe that just as there is life in nature there is death in nature, and that behind both these events are fundamental forces of nature at work.

Initially he believed only in the life instinct or life force which he used to call 'Eros' however over time he conceptualized a death instinct or a death force he called 'Thanatos'. He arrived at the concept of the death instinct from four considerations,

a) Relishing of pain by many of patients which put an end to the erstwhile pleasure principle

b) The tendency of the patients to maintain whatever state they were in be it pleasure or pain

c) The philosophical and scientific fact that every system wishes to preserve its state and almost yearns to re-establish its earlier state if its state is changed. This applied to human evolution would imply that from matter came life, from life mind and so there would be a tendency for the mind system to return to life system and for the life system to return to a state of matter.

d) The tendency of self destruction and directing it (the tendency) on others leading to destruction of the other

The above considerations led him to conceptualize two fundamental forces of nature at work in human psyche, the life instinct 'Eros' and the death instinct 'Thanatos'

30. What is 'The Project'?

Freud believed that over time as medical science would develop, a neurological basis would be found for the discoveries of Psychoanalysis and that would really make Psychoanalysis a rigorous science. He ventured on this enterprise to find a scientific foundation for Psychoanalysis and this attempt was titled 'The Project'. He could never finish 'The Project'.

31. Was Freud himself psychologically healthy?

Not completely. He was neurotic for seven years of his life, the period he calls as 'splendid isolation'. It was in this period, in the process of analyzing and healing himself he discovered many principles of Psychoanalysis.

Across his life he was never completely free from psycho-pathology and always had some psycho-pathology or the other. On the other hand he had a very happy married life and a very productive work life and so according to his own definition of mental health 'to be able to work and love', he was a reasonably healthy man.

Could he but free himself from all psycho-pathology using his own knowledge? The answer is No.

32. How did Freud view human nature?

Freud's view of human nature was greatly shaped by his personal and conceptual experience of the World War II. He was himself an atheist and a materialistically oriented thinker and the war led him to even more pessimism. He became very pessimistic about human nature and human future. He felt the goal of Psychoanalysis and of human enterprise in general was minimization of insanity and pain and to make 'unbearable unhappiness of life bearable'. One sees in him more of a Schopenhauer and less of a Voltaire. There was no great future awaiting humanity and no happy heavens either on earth or hereafter.

33. Is Freud today 'an atmosphere of opinion', a Weltanschauung?

Yes indeed so. Freud influences us in a variety of areas in ways we don't even know. Disciplines viz. neurology, psychiatry, psychology, sociology, economics, film studies, anthropology, cultural studies, art studies and management have been influenced by Freudian Ideas. Within Psychoanalysis Freud's ideas of the unconscious, repression, primary of childhood and significance of dreams are definitional to Psychoanalysis.

The expanse of Freud is extensive and pervasive. He is no longer held to be either infallible or comprehensive. Yet he remains an anchor reference even today for many a discourse where it comes to agree or disagree. It is easy to agree or disagree but the sin of omission is not easy to commit against Freud.

34. What are the good resources on Freud to know more on him?

Freud himself is a delight to read but one can start with books by Anthony Storr on Freud. An introductory book by Brenner can follow Anthony Storr. Once past Brenner one can read Freud in original and a number of good websites are available. The 'Cambridge Companion on Freud' is a good collection of writings on Freud.

35. How is Freud seen after so many years?

He is seen as the founding father of Psychoanalysis. The fundamental discoveries he made of the unconscious mind, the defenses at work, interpretation of dreams, and the therapy setting have stood the test of time. Some of his concepts are partially accepted today and some have been rejected. On the whole however he remains unquestionably in the gallery of geniuses.

We are never so defenseless against suffering, as when we love -   Sigmund Freud

Carl Jung

when I let go of what I am, I become what I might be- Lao Tzu

1. **Who was he?**

   Carl Jung was a Swiss psychiatrist who became disciple of Sigmund Freud and contributed enormously to Psychoanalysis, first as Freud's disciple and then as his critic and an independent analyst.

2. **What is his contribution to Psychoanalysis?**

   Jung gave to Psychoanalysis a completely new school of Psychoanalysis, the Jungian school (now also referred to as 'analytic psychology'). He gave a new model of the mind, the concept of collective unconscious and archetypes. He also gave a new method of dream interpretation and a new technique of therapy.

3. **What are his major works?**

   Jung wrote extensively on a variety of subjects. Some of his writings are,

   a) Man and his symbols
   b) Memoirs, Dreams, Reflections
   c) Psychological Types
   d) Synchronicity
   e) Alchemical Studies
   f) Four Archetypes
   g) Psychology and Alchemy
   h) The undiscovered self
   i) Psychology of the unconscious and some more
   j) Journal Recordings : The blue book, The Red book

4. **Why did Jung separate from Freud?**

   The two men were very different people in terms of personality and background and it was inevitable that someday they would separate. Jung felt too stifled and constrained under Freud who had become rigid with regard to his fundamental principles of Psychoanalytic theory.

   Conceptually Jung did not agree that Oedipus complex was universal and that it was the core cause of psychopathology. As time went by Jung also came to believe that the human unconscious is not only a personal entity but that below the personal unconscious that Freud had discovered lay a collective unconscious which stored evolutionary heritage of mankind.

Jung also differed from Freud that sexuality was the most important aspect in psychic functioning and he also created a different technique of dream analysis which was quite different from that of Freud although he used many of Freud's concepts of dream interpretation. Jung never disagreed on the existence of unconscious, the primacy of childhood or importance of dreams but his approach to the psyche apart from these agreements with Freud, was very different.

Philosophically also the two men were very different, Freud was an atheist materialist while Jung was a believer in search of the sacred and a meaning of life. The two had to separate some day and for Jung the day came not too soon.

5. What is Jung's model of the mind?

    Jung developed a model of the mind very different from Freud's. Jung's model of the mind is depicted below.

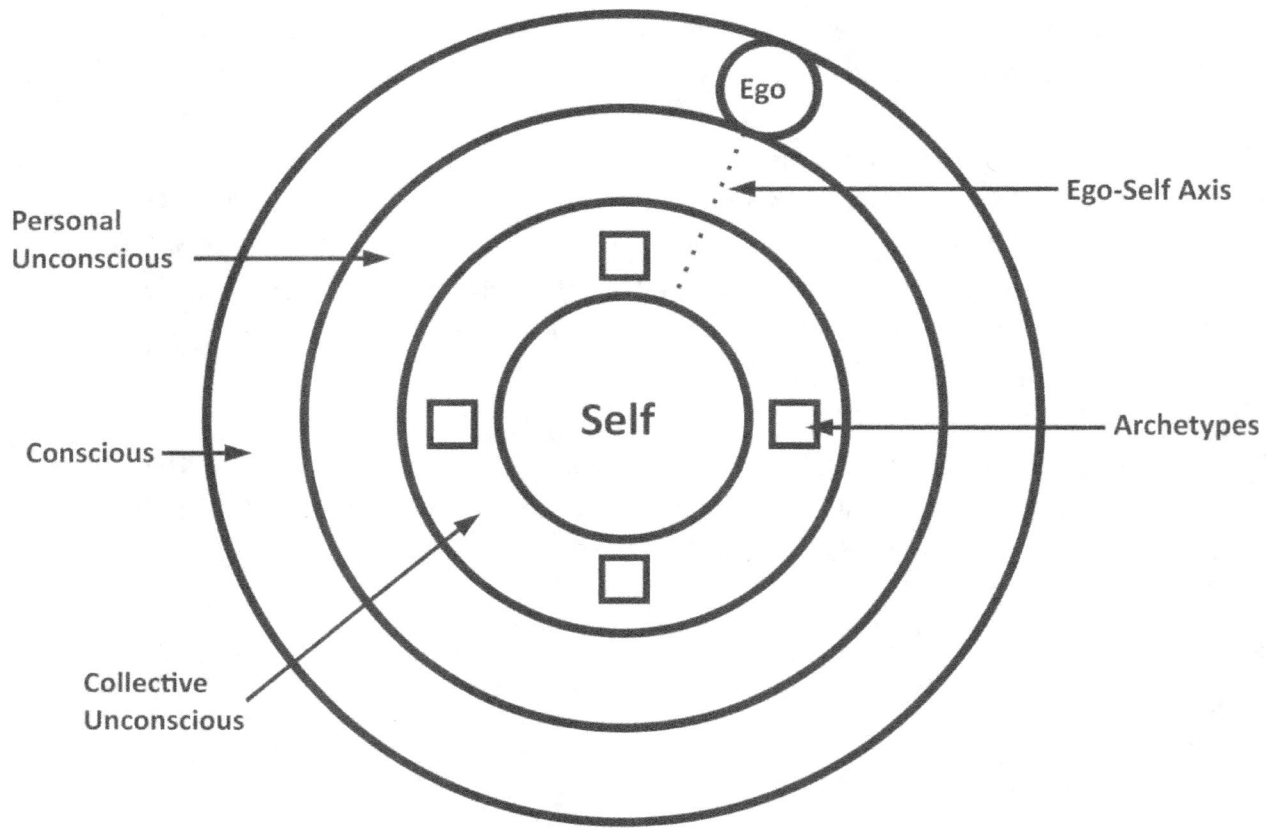

JUNG'S MODEL OF THE MIND

The Self is at the centre of the model and the Self can't be directly known but it is there governing the psyche. Outside of the Self is the collective unconscious constituted of collective heritage of the race and archetypes. The archetypes are the active psychological entities which are activated at appropriate time to initiate psychic action and allow one to play the psychological and social role at right stage of one's life. The layer outside the collective unconscious is the personal unconscious and outside of it is the conscious mind with the ego. The ego-self axis is a very important aspect of the psyche, any weakening of this axis creates psychological difficulties.

6. **What is the collective unconscious?**

For Jung the unconscious had two layers, the layer of personal unconscious that Freud had discovered and below it a layer of Collective Unconscious. The personal unconscious was constituted of psychic content specific to the individual however the collective unconscious was constituted of the evolutionary heritage of mankind and genetically present archetypes. The learning of the human race is thus not lost but is present in our unconscious and the archetypes are genetically present psychological entities that constitute the psychic frame in which we interpret and respond to the world. The archetypes also constitute the elemental motivational entities that make us enter the world to satisfy our purposes.

Because of the collective unconscious human beings who have never met end up having similar symbols in dreams and cultures that have never met have similar creations in the areas of literature, mythology, paintings and traditions.

The collective unconscious contains the life and society in potential form. We come into this world pre-supposing a 'type of world' and a 'type of life' and a 'type of society' unique to our species. Just as we enter the world pre-supposing the type of food our body can digest will be available similarly we also enter the world pre-supposing there will be parents, community, society and goals of life. Our entire being both biological and psychological is inherently structured for an 'expected environment'. The expected environment is expected to have the mother, the father, the old wise man, the predator, the magician, the saint, the warrior, the teacher and the healer. The human being is born expecting an expected human existence. The 'programme of life' and 'individuation' is nothing but realization in the individual's life the natural programme of the race, contextualized to the unique specificity of the individual.

7. **What are Archetypes?**

Archetypes are the active entities in the collective unconscious. The self through the archetypes regulates the programme of life. At the right time appropriate archetypes are activated by the Self. Thus when one is a child and sees the mother the mother archetype is activated, there is a comparison of this image in the collective unconscious and the real mother and correspondingly in the personal unconscious psychic entities related to the mother are created. As one grows old the 'old wise man' archetype is activated to help one fulfill the new role in life and society.

There are many archetypes that are present in the collective unconscious some of the main archetypes are, The mother, The Father, The Anima. The Animus, The Magician, The Saint, The Teacher, The Healer, The Persona, The Shadow and The old wise man

Archetypes appear close to Plato's 'Ideas' but there are differences between the two. Platonic Ideas are not human species dependent but Archetypes are strictly 'a human race entity', Platonic Ideas don't seek their fulfillment (they are more stoic) whereas Archetypes actively self their self fulfillment, the Platonic Ideas are not driven by a human Self whereas Archetypes in an individual are driven by his Self. Lastly Archetypes are evolutionary entities dynamic and evolving with evolution unlike the eternal steady and stoic platonic ideas.

8. **What is the Persona and the Shadow?**

Each of us has two parts to our personality, one which we know of (a part of which we show to society) and second part which is hidden in our unconscious (all that we don't like in ourselves we have pushed there).

That part of ourself we like to see and present to society is our Persona and the part of us we don't like to see or share with others, which we have pushed out of our awareness into our unconscious is our Shadow.

The Shadow often comes in our dreams as a dark or a black figure.

9. **What is the anima and the animus?**

Both of them are archetypes. Anima refers to the feminine part of us and Animus refers to the masculine part of us. All of us have both anima and animus.

Jung believed in the principle of compensation. The principle of compensation suggests that if in any part of the personality, say the conscious part, if masculinity is too high then in the unconscious part of the personality, say in dreams, femininity will be high inorder to maintain balance. Thus in this example anima and animus are kept in some balance by the psyche, between the waking and dream states according to the principle of compensation (which itself is a specific instance of 'balance' in nature, in human beings called homeostasis)

10. **What is Individuation?**

For Jung, the purpose of life was to realize one's potential. The Self was responsible to ensure that the individual was able to travel the journey innately embedded in his Self, which for him was his 'programme of life'. To become what is latent in us and what we are destined to develop into is Individuation. It is a process of becoming what we ought to become. Lack of fulfillment or pathology occurs when the individual is not able to individuate owing to reasons of constitutional difficulties, wrong experiences, accidents or wrong thinking (conscious or unconscious).

11. What type of patient's best benefit from Jungian therapy?

Patients who are searching for a meaning in their lives, patients who feel very close to nature and to arts in general and who are visually very imaginative and patients who are facing problems arising out of collective unconscious (ofcourse only if you believe in it) are the ones who stand to gain the most out of Jungian therapy.

12. **What were the differences in the approach of Freud and Jung?**

There were many differences between the two, some of which were,

a) Jung had developed his own model of the mind very different from Freud's model of the mind

b) Jung did not believe that sexuality was as important as Freud felt it was in the functioning of human psyche

c) Jung did not believe that Oedipus complex was universal and as important in psycho-pathology as Freud suggested it was

d) Jung did not believe in 5 days a week therapy, for him it was maximum 3 days a week slowly reduced to 1 day per week

e) Jung did not believe completely in Freud's technique of dream interpretation and he developed his own technique (called active imagination)

f) Jung didn't believe the unconscious was a personal entity but that below the personal unconscious was the collective unconscious which had evolved in the context of the collective experiences of the human race

g) Philosophically Freud was a materialist and Jung an Icealist

h) Freud was an atheist whereas Jung was a believer

i) Freud had a habit of searching for causes and Jung had a personality more concerned with finding the purpose, it was ontology versus teleology

j) Freud kept his research interest broadly limited to Psychoanalysis but Jung ventured far and wide into occult, culture, religion and mythology in addition to Psychoanalysis

13. How is technique different in Jungian therapy compared to Freudian therapy?

Jung felt that Freudian technique of being on the couch and constantly interpreting in terms of infantile events infact led people to regress far more than was necessary and it didn't strengthen enough the adult in them, rather it more often than not weakened the adult in patients. So Jung started seeing patients face to face.

He also felt 2-3 days per week was enough unlike 5 days a week of Freudian analysis. Also Jung would taper off number of sessions per week and as the patient felt better, number of sessions per week was reduced, to avoid dependency on therapist and promote independent strength of the patient which again was unlike Freud who continued with 5 days a week across the therapy.

Jung's dream analysis was also very different from Freud's approach to Dream analysis.

14. **How was Jung's approach to Dream analysis different from that of Freud?**
Jung had a radically different approach to Dream analysis compared to Freud and some of the differences were,

a) Jung (unlike Freud) interpreted the dreams at three levels, in the personal context of the dreamer, in the cultural context and in the archetypal context.

Freud never had such a model, he interpreted the dream based on his technique of dream interpretation which in Jung's approach would be only stage one of interpreting only in the personal context with a slight overlap of stage two of interpreting in the cultural context. Freud never believed in the concept of the collective unconscious or the archetypes and so interpreting the dream in any of those terms did not arise

b) Jung felt all dreams were not dreams of wish fulfillment or trauma (as Freud believed) and there were many dreams which were actually related to present or future course of life without any content of pathology in them

c) Jung felt there were many dreams where the manifest content was the same as latent content and there no interpretation was needed (unlike Freud), rather what was needed was an understanding of what the dream meant for the life of the dreamer

d) Jung felt rather than reducing the manifest dream to the latent content (Freud's approach) what was a better approach was to develop the dream, a technique he called active imagination where the patient develops and amplifies the dream for the purpose of dream analysis

e) Jung also felt that many symbols in the dream come from the collective unconscious and so the dream interpretation had to factor in the aspects of the collective unconscious and the archetypes, something quite distinct from Freud

f) The interpretation of symbols that Jung was different from that of Freud. Jung saw much less of sexuality, aggression and fear behind the symbols compared to Freud

15. What is active imagination?

Active imagination is a part of the Jungian technique of dream analysis where the dreamer is asked to develop the dream for the purpose of dream analysis.

16. What is 'the stroke of noon'?

The age of 35 signifies the midpoint of human life and to that Jung referred to as 'the stroke of the noon'. Before 35 according to Jung, the human life is the life of passion, adventure and acquisition and after 35 is the life of culture, creation and giving back to society. Often a reversal of values happens in this zone of human age.

If a healthy psyche is not there, ready to accept the inevitable change at this age and joyfully enter the second part of life, mortality, uncertainty, unfulfilled desires, fears, anger, pain and disappointment overwhelm the individual leading to a mid-life crisis often bringing in depression. For many individuals, the mid-life crisis in a psychic sense becomes a second puberty phase where earlier unresolved issues emerge with great intensity.

17. What are the personality types?

Jung in his observation of people found that between any two human beings there are commonalities and differences. The differences contribute to our uniqueness and the commonalities allow us to assign people into groups or 'types'.

Jung divided people first into two types, the introverts and the extroverts and then within each type he created four sub-types the sensing type, the thinking type, the feeling type and the intuitive type. Thus overall he divided people into 8 types. The 8 personality types would be; introverted sensing type, introverted feeling type, introverted thinking type, introverted intuitive type, extroverted sensing type, extroverted feeling type, extroverted thinking type and extroverted intuitive type,

Each type had a particular way of viewing the world, specific strengths, weaknesses, a predisposition to certain psycho-pathology and a natural fitness for certain professions and roles in society. The MBTI inventory so popularly used today for educational and career counseling is based on Jung's personality types.

18. Was Jung influenced by Indian Psychology and Philosophy?

Jung was greatly interested in culture, religion, philosophy and the occult. He had fascination for Indian psychology and philosophy, however I don't believe he could grasp in depth the Indian philosophy or psychology. He did try to integrate into this thinking the Indian knowledge however it remains a superficial effort evident to anyone who has been deep into Indian philosophy and psychology. However his interest and entry did provide respectability to ancient Indian knowledge and extended an invitation to scholars which is as yet open.

19. What is the 'search of the sacred'?

Jung felt Freud had over estimated the significance of sexuality in the human psyche. Jung's idea was that the modern man is more in search of the sacred which he has lost than he is in search of sexual pleasure. Freud in Jung's view had tried in vain to substitute the search of the sacred with sex and elevated Psychoanalysis based on sexuality and aggression to the status of a new religion. In Jung's view the modern man is in search of cultural rootedness, a way of reconnecting to nature, a search of the sacred and in the ultimate analysis a 'meaning that can provide purpose to the banality of life'.

20. What is the Red book and the Blue book?

Jung wrote extensively in the form of books and journals. The Red book and the Blue book are the journals he wrote and they carry a wealth of his writings. The scope ranges from observations, comments, personal experiences and an attempt at understanding the occult. The Red book especially contains his journey across his psychosis, the period like Freud's 'splendid isolation' what Jung would call 'nekia'. Initially only one of the two was published but now both are available to readers and scholars.

21. What is 'the programme of life'?

Jung believed that just as we come into this world prepared to find the type of food we can digest and survive, in a psychological sense we come prepared to find a world where there would be parent, siblings, friends, colleagues, relatives and so on. That is we come into this world prepared for a web of psychological relationships and a social format of life. The format of life which can't change in essence but can change only in specifics for the human race (so far as our biology is the same) is called by Jung as 'the programme of life'. It says that our life is a sequential programme of being a child, the prince, the hunter-gatherer, the parent and the old wise man.

The expressions of this basic programme change over history but in essence the programme of life remains unchanged for the human race. Today hunting is substituted by a job or a business and the old wise man part by a post retirement non-profit activity, however in essence the programme is the same. A readiness and ability to live according to the programme of life brings a sense of naturalness, rootedness and a sense of accomplishment and fulfillment.

22. What was Jung's approach to the old age?

Jung believed that the old age is not only to wait for death filled with anxiety but that the old age is to be lived fully and purposefully as much as any other stage of life. The old age has its own purpose and that is to provide society and the next generation with care and wisdom of life. He himself lived that role, to put it in his archetypal language, the role of 'the old wise man of Kusnatch'

23. What are 'the healing images'?

Jung discovered that as healing happens in therapy the communication of healing often comes to the patient in the form of images and not words. Often the patient is able to think difficult things in terms of images. These visuals that come up in the patient's mind and are associated with healing in some way (either helping in healing or communicating that healing is happening) are called the healing images.

24. What is the significance of Mandala?

Mandalas are geometric figures (Yantras) used in ancient Hindu mysticism and spirituality. Jung saw the Mandala from Psychotherapy standpoint. The geometric forms of the Mandala occurred to people spontaneously across the world without any formal training and these geometric shapes were seen in every culture. These forms for him symbolized something in the collective unconscious and were of deep significance in what they were trying to symbolize and say.

Jung never went into 'mantra' and occult practices that are closely related to Mandala, however what was interesting to him was how patients in the process of healing spontaneously used to draw linear geometric shaped Mandala and then somehow round them. The principle of compensation, balanced development, healing and individuation was at work sending communication on the psyche and the programme of life through these geometric figures. It was psyche drawing itself.

25. What is Synchronicity?

Jung believed there was a relatedness between events that seem on the surface not to be causally connected and yet their occurrence leaves one in awe of something we pass off as co-incidence, luck or 'it just happens'. To Jung there were no meaningless co-incidences. There was a 'deeper relation of meaning' if not of 'causality' between such events.

Jung defines Synchronicity as 'temporally coincident occurrences of acausal events'. Events connected at a deeper layer of reality although on the surface having no causal connection. He had extensive discussions with Einstein and Pauli and he became convinced of a deeper connect of reality than is visible to us. He felt this 'deeper connect of reality' was yet to be scientifically discovered and it was there that in scientific terms perhaps explanations to his concepts of collective unconscious and archetypes can be found.

Some of the events which we all experience and which we can try to explain using the concept of synchronicity are given here,

a) Knowing something will happen and it happens (and we are not referring to ordinarily predictable events)
b) Two things happening at the same time (you start thinking about somebody exactly when he thinks of you and both of you can cross-verify the timings)
c) A strange feeling of 'having been there' although you have been to a place for the first time
d) A strange feeling of 'having met before' although you have met someone for the first time

26. In what countries is Jungian therapy popular?
Jungian therapy is popular in Europe and USA, however in small groups it has adherents and admirers in practically every country where Psychotherapy is firmly established.

27. How was Jung's personal life? Did he have affairs with his patients?
Jung was happily married to his wife with kids. He did have affairs with many of his patients and two of such affairs became public, one with Ms. Tony Wolf and the other with Ms. Sabrina Spielberg. Some popular films have been made on these affairs, as I call them, 'intimate matters of intricate nature'.

28. Did Jung become Psychotic in some phase of his life? What is Nekiya?

Yes sometime after his break with Freud, Jung did turn psychotic and this phase continued for quite some years. He noted down all he experienced and thought during this phase in his writings. When this phase ended Jung returned with redoubled positivity and energy to work. Jung called this period of his psychosis as Nekiya. In his view such a period of dis-orientation (be it neurotic or psychotic) is experienced by many people and when they come out of it they inwardly feel as if they have a purpose, a mission to fulfill in life and they life a more alive, productive and a creative life of purpose and fulfillment.

29. What are good resources to know more on Jung?

Jung is not an easy writer to read. One can start with books by Anthony Stevens on Jung. Follow it up with a number of good websites which are available free. Once past this one can read Jung in the original. The Cambridge companion on Jung is a good collection of papers on Jung.

30. How is Jung seen today?

Many of Jung's ideas have not been empirically proved and the Jungian therapy is no longer the hot therapy of the season. However a large group of analysts and people do believe here is a great value in Jung's ideas and approach to therapy. His 'personality types' is widely used in the areas of education and management. His work on symbols is still being explored to understand the area of visuals and meaning. One of the central difficulty with his work is that much of it is not within the range current scientific research. People and analysts who have an opening and an interest in art, culture, anthropology and occult have great admiration for Jung. Jungian Psychotherapy continues to occupy an important position among the top 25 psychotherapies in the world.

Show me a sane man and I will cure him for you - Carl Jung

Melanie Klein

Silence is a source of great strength - Lao Tzu

1) Who was Melanie Klein?

Ms. Melanie Klein was a psychoanalyst who founded the Kleinien school of Psychoanalysis. Ms. Klein worked for most part in Britain where she founded the school. To this day, Britain continues to be the global center of the Kleinien School. 'Tavistock' (in Britain) continues to be the most respected centre for Kleinien School of psychoanalysis in the world today.

2) What are her major works?

Ms. Klein wrote quite many books and papers. The most well-known of her writings are,

a) Envy and Gratitude
b) Love, Hate and Reparation
c) Psychoanalysis of Children
d) Narrative of a child analysis
e) Selected Papers of Melanie Klein

3) What are the major differences between the Freudian and Kleinien theory?

Ms. Klein created her theory and therapy from her work with children unlike Freud who worked far less with children. Freud had created the picture of the psyche of the child based upon analysis of adults who had regressed. Ms. Klein did extensive direct 'child observation' on which she based her theory and therapy. Ms. Klein while she accepted broadly the fundamental principles of Psychoanalysis (ofcourse discovered by Freud) her approach to theory and therapy was quite different.

With respect to the development of the psyche in childhood, she emphasized **Positions and not Stages**, the difference being that while stages were age related (with a clear beginning and an end) positions are a psychic orientation one can take at any point of time in one's life. The positions (explained later) she came up with were the **paranoid schizoid position** and the **depressive position**. Across one's life one can at any time enter into a paranoid schizoid position or a depressive position. The paranoid schizoid position is a pathological and infantile position while the depressive position is a healthy and mature position. Infants start with a paranoid schizoid position and then they have to move into a depressive position inorder to institute a healthy psyche.

Klein also believed that super-ego was innate in human beings and it did not need a resolution of Oedipus complex for the super-ego to come into existence. Klein also pushed back the onset of the Oedipus complex to about 2-2.5 years much earlier than Freud had stated it to be at 4-7 years of age. Klein also developed considerably the play therapy for children.

4) **What is the paranoid schizoid position?**

Klein said that the infant does not understand the concepts of presence and absence. For the infant the breast that gives him milk, warmth, emotional touch and security is thought of as the good breast. When the infant is hungry and the breast is not available, the infant believes a bad breast is present (since he can't understand the concept of absence). The infant in fantasy attacks the bad breast since it doesn't give it milk, warmth, emotional touch and security (like the good breast). However despite the attack when the infant realizes he has not been able to destroy the bad breast and bring back the good breast, the infant recognizes the power of the bad breast and his own powerlessness against it.

The infant (now) post his attack on the bad breast is terrified of the prospect that bad breast will attack back, torture and destroy him just as he had desired to do to the bad breast. This creates a paranoid fear in the infant.

However after some time when the good breast reappears and offers him milk, warmth, love and security the infant is pleased and secure. However the infant doesn't realize the good and the bad breast are the same. The infant in his fantasy keeps the two entities the good breast and the bad breast separate.

This psychological position where the good and the bad breast are felt as being completely separate entities, the good breast being completely good and the bad breast being completely bad, is called the paranoid schizoid position. It (position) is so called because in this position there is paranoia of attack from the bad breast and a schizoid tendency at work to keep the good and the bad breast separate. The paranoid schizoid position lasts till 4- 6 months of age.

5) **What is the depressive position?**

Over a period of time the infant realizes that the good and the bad breast are not different but one and the same and that is an issue of presence and absence. This leads the infant to in his mind combine the all positive good breast with the all negative bad breast to arrive at a realistic understanding of the breast that is that the breast in reality which is both present and absent and is neither all good nor all bad but is a mixture of good and bad like everything else in reality.

This position however of recognizing the real breast (which is a mixture of good and bad) leads to a depression because now the infant no longer has the 'all good breast'. The 'high' it (the infant) used to feel while having the all good breast, can't be felt anymore. At the same time the absolute badness of the bad breast is also not felt and the paranoia, of murderous and torturous attack from the bad breast, is also not there. However the infant doesn't value the cessation of paranoia as much it values the loss of the absolute high (pleasure) and so it goes into a depression (temporary).

This position is called the depressive position. The infant now feels guilty that it had attacked the breast thinking of it as being all bad which was not true. This guilt leads the infant to undertake 'reparation' in fantasy by trying to repair the breast and do 'good' to it. The depressive position is attained between 6-9 months (in some children between 4-6 months)

Ms. Klein created this theory from direct infant observation and therapy of numerous child patients. Over time the good and the bad breast become 'templates' and 'metaphors' and yet the essential intra-psychic childhood drama keeps repeating itself across life.

6) **What is reparation?**
The infant when it comes to realize that the breast it attacked, thinking of it as the bad breast was infact not a bad breast, the infant feels guilt and tries to undo the damage it has inflicted upon the breast. This act of making up is called reparation. In Klienien terms this is the first purposive act of creativity.

7) **What is 'envy' in the Kleinien scheme of things?**
Envy relates to being unable to tolerate anything good that is outside of oneself. Every human being has envy at every stage of his life, be it less or more. Envy for Klein is a very strong psychic entity which is innately present in human beings. Envy is one of the most repressed entities and in Klienien analysis unless envy comes up in analysis, it (analysis) has not gone deep enough.

The infant feels envy against the good breast since the good breast has -in the infant's belief- all the goodness and richness of the world. The infant believes the good breast is holding back and hoarding all the goodness. The infant also feels it is humiliating to be 'dependent' on the good breast (which is a narcissistic injury). Hence the infant driven primarily by envy, attacks the good breast. Over time however, the infant feels guilt about the 'attack of envy'.

The infant thus attacks the bad breast out of anger and the good breast out of envy.

(Some Kleiniens believe, at times we attack even the goodness within us and so there is an intra-self envy also)

8) **What is 'greed' in the Kleinien scheme of things?**
Greed like envy, is yet another entity innate in human infants. The infant feels greed when it sees the good breast having all the goodness in itself. The greed leads the infant to fantasy (or phantasy) of robbing the good breast and appropriate all the goodness that is there in the good breast. The attack of greed may often accompany the attacks of envy.

9) **What is the difference between Fantasy and Phantasy?**
Fantasy is the conscious imagination, be it wish-fulfilling or traumatic. Phantasy is the unconscious imagination, be it wish-fulfilling or traumatic. It is difficult for many to believe that we can indulge in unconscious wishful imagination, however in therapy it distinctly comes out that we all behold phantasies of which we were never aware.

10) **What is a part object?**
The infant in very early part of his life doesn't understand that the breast is a part of the mother's body and that the mother is a complete individual with desire, mind and autonomy of her own. The infant feels the breast is an independent separate part that exists by itself. This understanding about the breast of the infant is called part object understanding. The infant thus initially understands only part objects and not full objects. As adults we often like only certain limited parts of some person and we are unable to accept the full person as he is. This is essentially a part object approach to the person and maturity lies in the full object understanding and acceptance.

11) **What is the concept of the 'good mother' and the 'bad mother'?**

The child often goes into the paranoid schizoid position and in that position thinks about the mother being completely good or completely bad. In phantasy too often there are good mother and bad mother imago. The good and bad mother images can happen only after the child has graduated from part object understanding to a full object understanding. At work place often people label some colleague as being all good or all bad. The unconscious template at work there is of the good mother and the bad mother. The defense in operation is splitting.

12) What is Projection?

When we have thoughts and feelings unacceptable to our morality or ego, we attribute them on to others. If X is envious about Y, he may feel that infact Y is envious about X. This psychological phenomenon is called projection. Projection is a very common defense employed by both normal and pathologica individuals and especially by children.

13) What is Projective Identification?

Severely regressed or pathological individuals often have a unique ability to make you feel what they are feeling (when you are with them). Thus if they are angry you will start feeling anger in their company. (Generally the feelings so transferred into you are unconscious in the person and he is not aware that he has such feelings). This psychological phenomenon is called projective identification.

Projective identification is both a defense and a mode of communication.

In therapy of severe psychotic patients the therapist experiences projective identification many times. There is also something called delayed projective identification where some hours after the patient has left, the therapist feels what the patient had put into him. How this happens is not clear but that it happens is not in doubt.

14) How is Kleinien Psychotherapy different from the Freudian Psychotherapy?

Kleinien Psychotherapy works more in transference than classical Freudian Psychotherapy. The Kleinien Psychotherapy focuses more on the attainment of the depressive position, resolution of envy, greed and reparation. The Freudian therapy focuses more on resolution of Oedipal issues. One way to describe it is that the Freudian approach is more an Eros driven approach while the Kleinien approach is more of an aggression driven approach. The Freudian therapy is good for Oedipal pathology whereas the Kleinien approach is good for pre-Oedipal pathologies. The Kleinien approach also places more emphasis on fantasy and phantasy (and thereby on the individual's constitution) compared to the Freudian approach.

15) Where do you get trained in Kleinien Psychotherapy?

There are centers of Kleinien Psychotherapy across the world and one has to get enrolled there, undergo training analysis, see patients under supervision and write papers as per the requirements of IPS (International Psychoanalytic Society) to become a Kleinien psychotherapist.

16) Who are the major Kleinien thinkers after Klein?

Hanna Segal, Betty Joseph, Esther Bick, Donald Meltzer, Herbert Rosenfield, Wilfred Bion (if can I say it) are some of the leading Kleinien thinkers after Klein.

17) What are the major sources to learn about Klein?

One can start with introductory books by Hanna Segal. One can then move to books in their original by Klein. Thereafter one can take up papers by leading Kleinien thinkers. Some resourceful websites especially the website of the 'Kleinien trust' are also good resources to study on Klein.

18) What problems are more suited for Kleinien therapy rather than for Freudian therapy?

Kleinien therapy is more officious in pre-oedipal pathologies relating to very early problems in object relations. Some paranoid patients for whom the issue is the impending attack of the bad breast benefit a great deal from Kleinien therapy. Similarly for some depression patients for whom the central issue is loss of the good breast can also benefit from Kleinien therapy.

19) Does Kleinien theory give more importance to the patient's constitution compared to environment?

In a way yes, since for Klein the unconscious phantasy of the child was more important, than the actual behavior of people, in the child's environment. The nature and intensity of the unconscious phantasy depends primarily on the child's constitution. Two infants who miss the mother for two hours don't respond the same way to the absence of the mother. So yes, for Klein though she doesn't loudly say it, constitution is more important than environment in **relative** terms. This doesn't go on to take any extreme position that either constitution or environment doesn't matter. Ofcourse both matter.

20) What are the common pathological phantasies in the child's mind according to the Kleinien theory?

Some of the common pathological phantasies in the child's mind are,

a) Being swallowed by the big mother
b) Being robbed by the mother of all the precious things the child has
c) Entering the mother's womb and killing the babies there
d) Robbing the good breast of all the goodness and richness it has
e) Attacking the bad breast out of anger and the good breast out of envy to blow them to pieces

21) **What are the Kleinien explanations for some common psychological problems?**

In Kleinien terms paranoia is explained as the fear of the attack of the bad breast which is completely different from the Freudian explanation based on homosexuality. The Kleinien explanation of mania rests on getting one with the good breast in contrast to the Freudian explanation of sudden release of libido pent up (locked) in depression or (repressed) anxiety.

22) What is object relations school in Psychoanalysis? Is the Kleinien School an object relations school?

The object relations schools emphasize more on the object representations in the mind and the relations between them, in contrast to drive oriented schools which emphasize the conflict between the drive and defense. The Kleinien School is an object relations school in Psychoanalysis.

23) **Have there being important analysts who have been through both Freudian and Kleinien analysis?**

Yes Guntrip and Wilfred Bion were two of the many analysts who had been through both Freudian and Kleinien analysis.

24) Was Melanie Klein herself healthy and happy person?

Klein had a very difficult life and she herself suffered from depression for a long time. She was healthy in a sense that she could accomplish so much in the area of psychotherapy. However her relationships with her daughters were hardly what one call 'happy'. It seems she was reasonably healthy but not quite happy.

25) **In what countries is Klienien Psychotherapy popular?**

Klein is popular in Britain, Europe, Latin America and partly in India and USA.

One of the many interesting and surprising experiences of the beginner in child analysis is to find in even very young children, a capacity for insight, which is often far greater than that of adults - Melanie Klein

Wilfred Bion

free from desire, you realize the mystery - Lao Tzu

1) Who was Wilfred Bion?
Wilfred Bion was a psychoanalyst who pioneered new concepts in the area of Psychoanalysis creating a framework and a school of his own. Wilfred Bion was born in India to his British parents. Wilfred Bion served in the army and won awards before he entered Psychoanalysis. One of the defining moments came in the army when his unit was engaged in difficult tank battle, face to face with death. Bion's unit won the battle but Bion had a first-hand occasion to see human behavior under extreme crisis and it created a lasting impression on him. Wilfred Bion was one of the few psychoanalysts who worked with groups.

2) What are the major works of Wilfred Bion?
A Memoir of the future, Experiences in Groups and other Essays, Elements of Psychoanalysis, Attention and Interpretation, Taming wild thoughts, Cogitations (A new extended edition), War Memoirs and many other books and papers constitute his works.

3) What are the concepts he contributed to Psychoanalysis?
Wilfred Bion contributed many original concepts to Psychoanalysis, some of which are; attacks on linking, the alpha and the beta elements, the alpha function, L (love) H (hate) K (knowledge) and −K (knowledge avoidance), the container, the contained and Psychoanalytic group dynamics.

4) Did Wilfred Bion undergo Psychoanalysis twice?
Yes he did, first with a Freudian analyst and then with a Kleinien analyst.

5) What is the Grid and the language Bion created to institute exactness in Psychoanalysis?
Bion felt the language of Psychoanalysis was too inexact and so he tried to bring in notations from mathematics for use in psychoanalytic discourse to make it exact. Using these notations he created 'The Grid'. Over time he abandoned the notations and the Grid and returned to the classical intuitive and descriptive discourse of Psychoanalysis.

6) What are the alpha and beta elements?

Bion classified the contents of the unconscious into two qualitative groups. First were those entities in the unconscious which were adequately processed in the unconscious and were ready for use in dreaming or fantasy and second were those entities in the unconscious which were as yet unprocessed or inadequately processed and so were not available for dream or fantasy. The first group of entities (adequately processed) he called the Alpha elements whereas the second group of entities (inadequately processed or not processed) he called the Beta elements.

7) What is the alpha function?

Alpha function is that psychic function which acts upon the beta elements to convert them into alpha elements so that they are available for dreaming and fantasy. Alpha elements have the possibility of moving upwards from the unconscious to the conscious (even if post disguise) however the beta elements don't have such a potential and so are thrown outwards rather than moving upwards. Health depends on reducing the quantum and intensity of the beta elements and converting them into alpha elements. Thus the alpha function is critical to psychic health.

8) What is L, H, K and –K?

Bion during a period in his life, started using notations like in mathematics because he felt Psychoanalysis was too inexact. He also tried to create a grid to make conceptualization more exact but over time abandoned it. L, K, H, -K were notations used by Bion during this period. L is love, H is hate, K is knowledge and –K is an active avoidance of knowledge.

Bion felt that in therapy one has to move from love and hate to knowledge that can bring insight and transformation. Thus in therapy one has to move from L and H to K if healing has to happen. However –K is the entity that opposes K (knowledge) and thereby healing. -K is not only a passive resistance but it actively tries to denude, strip, denigrate and destroy the knowledge that can bring in insight and transformation.

9) What is O?

O was the notation used by Bion for the 'inaffable', something that could not be seen or known but whose after effects can be felt. O was an emotional explosion which on the surface comes as 'transformation' or in a more diluted form of 'insight'. Bion's ineffable O is very near to Jung's transcendental function in terms of its effects although in ontological terms, O is a Kantian unknowable unlike the transcendental function. O doesn't always happen and so often goal of healing and transformation is not reached.

In his later days Bion attributed to the elusive O what he attributed in his early days to -K, the 'not happening' of transformation.

10) How does mind grow? How does Healing happen?

In Bion's view the mind grows in therapy when exposed to the 'truth'. This 'truth' is essentially an emotional experience. The growth of the mind and healing both for Bion are emotional experiences. Pure cognitive knowing without any emotional correlate can't bring in healing. In his later years he also attributed this growth and healing to the inaffable O.

11) What is Transformation?

Bion in the course of his experience realized that in therapy often the patient agrees to everything you say but nothing happens in terms of change because no emotional movement is happening. In Bion's words 'the interpretation is accepted but the premise is rejected'. The key focus has always to be on 'transformation' and in Bion's view it was —K that was opposing transformation in addition to envy, rage and other defenses. The inaffable O was helping transformation.

Infact 'transformation' involves apart from interpersonal dynamics, an intra-psychic structural situation and an energy dynamics, that awaits comprehension which can lead us to a more reliable understanding of 'transformation'.

12) What are the elements according to Bion which take part in projective identification?

According to Bion it is the beta elements which take part in projective identification.

13) What is meant by the 'container' and the 'contained'?

The infant according to Bion shows his aggression either directly or through projective identification to the mother who has to 'contain' that aggression and give it back to the child having converted it into something positive. So if the infant beats the mother with his small hands, the mother doesn't have to pay back in the same coin, rather the mother smiles at this and cuddles and loves the baby. What is happening here is that the infant is giving aggression which is not responded to with aggression, rather the mother not only contains aggression but gives it back as love and a smile. The mother here acts as a container (who contains aggression) and the child as the contained (whose aggression is contained).

Across life we all need containers and we all have to contain others when occasion demands. Thus when you go angry and shout there is some friend, who doesn't hit back but 'contains' your anger. Here you are the contained and the one who stays calm (your friend) while you are angry is the container.

14) What did Bion contribute to Group Therapy?

Bion did pioneering work of applying Psychoanalysis to groups which was a great leap because here we were moving from the micro (the individual) to the macro (the group). Bion worked extensively with groups to study people at work from Psychoanalytic perspective.

Bion found that when a group is given a task, the group starts existing in two modes. In one mode the group acts like a rational entity and dedicates itself to the task it is supposed to do. The state when the group is into, it is called as the 'work group'. However the same group often gets into a different state where the group behaves in a non-rational non-optimum way driven by psychopathology and works in strange ways that have little to do with attainment of the group task. This state when the group enters into, it is called the 'basic assumption group'.

15) What is the work group?

The group when it acts rationally focused on achieving its objective, it is called the work group. Any group behaves as a work group for some time and for some time as a basic assumptions group. In organizations it is a critical managerial skill to keep the group in the state of a 'work group'.

16) What is the basic assumption group?

The group when it acts in a non-productive pathological way, not aligned to attain its task, it is called the basic assumptions group. The basic assumptions group takes any of the three positions viz.,

a) Dependency	:	Where the group gives up initiative and becomes completely dependent on the leader
b) Fight – Flight	:	When the group is ready to fight or give up
c) Pairing	:	Where two people in the group (generally involving the leader as one of the two) carry on a conversation and decision making while others are a passive audience

In all the above three positions, the basic assumptions group acts in a pathological non-productive way. The ideal is to make the group develop insight on what is happening and take it back to the state of the work group.

17) What is 'attack on linking'? Why does 'attack on linking' happen?

Bion said that the key element in thinking is the 'link' between two thoughts or ideas and if this link was attacked it would render difficult the normal thinking process. Thus if any force attacked the linking of thoughts or ideas, it would bring in cognitive disorders.

'Attacks on linking' refers to the attacks that happen from the unconscious mind on the thoughts and ideas which results in cognitive disorders mostly of the psychotic type. It renders (in extreme situations) the thinking and speech of the person incoherent and often irrelevant.

For Bion the 'attack on linking' is owing to 'envy'. Since thoughts bring messages of 'good' out there in the world which one can't have, one destroys the very vehicle that brings such messages which are unbearable. Envy in Bion's view causes attacks on linking. In my personal opinion there is one more factor 'narcissistic rage' which can also cause attacks on linking, this narcissistic rage is 'a rage at the world because the world is not my world'.

18) What is 'maternal reverie' in Bionian thinking?

Bion's concept of 'maternal reverie' is that the mother is so attuned to the baby that she knows with partial or no communication from the baby what the baby is feeling or wants. This state of 'maternal reverie' is possible owing to some form of communication (of thoughts and feelings) between the infant and the mother, which we don't completely understand. Many people believe the state of maternal reverie continues at its peak till 9 months of age after which it starts weakening and doesn't remain as acute. Bion saw this state as a very fascinating state and much is to be learnt from it. For therapy Bion believed if the therapist could create this state in him, he can empathically know and feel much that the patient is undergoing but he doesn't say it and many times he doesn't even know it. The concept is very close to Winnicott's concept of 'primary maternal preoccupation' except that in spirit Bion's concept is a more passive and a more 'state of being' concept while Winnicott's concept is more of an 'activity and engagement' concept.

19) What is the state Bion wanted the therapist to enter the therapy room with?

Bion wanted to therapists to enter the therapy room 'without memory and desire' so that the therapist can actually act as a blank screen and look at therapy without any bias allowing for original and goalless insights to emerge in therapy. It is an endeavor to respond to free association with a free floating attention. The therapists free reach in search of the meaning of the patient's free expression.

20) How is Bion viewed within the Psychoanalytic community?

Bion (along with Lacan and Meltzer) is viewed within the Psychoanalytic community as one of those who are more in search of truth and less in search of healing. Bion is also viewed as a very original but a very difficult and abstruse thinker. Some call him as one of the most original thinkers in Psychoanalysis. Most analysts tend to agree that the respect due to Bion yet to be awarded and the assimilation of Bionian ideas into Psychoanalysis is awaiting its hour. Presently a strong movement is ongoing to assimilate Bion adequately in Psychoanalysis. Like Kierkegaard, Bion can perhaps say, 'only the day after tomorrow belongs to me'.

21) Can Bion's thoughts be applied for companies in the area of organizational behavior?

Yes ofcourse and it is being done by researchers and consultants though not on a mass scale or in a very popular way. The point is very few management researchers or consultants are familiar with Bionian ideas but as the ideas travel more, we should see more of Bion in the area of organizational behavior.

22) How does Bion stand in conceptual terms vis.a. vis Freud and Klein?

Bion never disputed the fundamental concepts discovered by Freud and Klein and infact he had a first-hand experience of both approaches as he underwent analysis twice, first with a Freudian analyst and then with a Kleinien analyst. Bion brought in new concepts to enrich existing theory and take theory in directions never thought of before. His work is very original and in spirit, it is 'enriching the existing' and not a critique of the existing.

23) Where is Wilfred Bion popular in terms of concepts and therapy?

Wilfred Bion is popular in Britain, some parts of Europe and some parts of USA. More and more analysts in India are slowly taking note of Bionian ideas to enrich their existing practice with it.

24) Which thinkers have carried forward the Bionian thinking?

Most notable are Neville Symington, S. H. Foulkes, Rickman, Bridger, Main and Patrick De Mare.

25) What are the resources on Bion?

Bion is hardly the person one should read on Bion. His writings are dense and abstruse. One can start with 'The clinical thinking of Wilfred Bion' by Neville Symington and 'A beam of intense darkness' by Grotstein. Post this one can move onto Bion in original and then one can take to papers on Bion. Online material on Bion is in abundance and some it really simple to read.

The purest form of listening is to listen without memory or desire – Wilfred Bion

Winnicott

from wonder into wonder existence opens - Lao Tzu

1) Who was Donald Winnicott?

Donald Winnicott was a British psychoanalyst. The British Psychoanalytic movement during that time (World War II and post war) got divided into three groups, the Freudians, the Kleiniens and the Independent group (which did not wish to join either group). Donald Winnicott became a leading figure of the Independent group.

2) How did Winnicott come to Psychoanalysis?

Donald Winnicott was trained as a pediatrician and in the course of treating children and infants, he got interested in the psychological aspects of the infant and thus started moving towards Psychoanalysis. One of his popular books is 'Through Pediatrics to Psychoanalysis: Collected Papers'. Winnicott's path, as an independent path in analysis, is based on collection of his work and insights and has a limited but distinct following of its own.

3) What school did he create in Psychoanalysis?

Winnicott pursued his unique path and his original thinking across his life. He proposed a set of ideas regarding the human mind and psycho-pathology. He wrote a number of very original papers and he practiced Psychotherapy in a very original way at times breaching the normal guidelines of Psychoanalysis.

4) How is Winnicott positioned vis-à-vis other Psychoanalytic thinkers?

He is seen as an independent Psychoanalytic thinker who was at ease leveraging ideas from either Freud or Klein, without belonging to either group and at the same time discovering his own original ideas. There is a simplicity and easy flow in his writings that speak of someone at ease with himself and the world, not eager to convince or convert anybody. He is regarded today as one of the most original psychoanalysts, a grounded practical person and a very good human being. When one reads Winnicott one feels he is one of the few in whom the aggression has been thoroughly neutralized by libido. He was one of the few 'school founding psychoanalysts' who in personal life was substantially healthy and happy.

5) What were his major conceptual contributions to Psychoanalysis?

He contribute many original ideas like, good enough mothering, the holding environment, true and false self, going on being, unorganisation and disintegration, transitional object, transitional space, creativity, wonder, the concept of Play and on being alive.

6) **What is good enough mothering?**

Winnicott believed that the child wants the mother to be an ideal mother, to be always available and infinitely giving without reserve or conditions. However no human mother can be such an ideal mother and so frustrations in the child are inevitable. Thus the expectation from the mother is not to be an ideal mother which no human mother can be, but rather to be a 'good enough mother' and provide a 'good enough mothering' so the child develop into a normal healthy happy individual.

When good enough mothering is not available, the child develops or gets predisposed to developing psycho-pathology. Winnicott brought to the centre stage the role of the mother in psychic health and psychopathology. Unlike Klein he gave less importance to fantasy or phantasy and more importance to the real life behavior of the mother. For him the containing element of the mother was of great importance apart from her being able to be alive and joyful in the dyad with the child. Winnicott used to strongly believe that absence of good enough mothering was a major causation factor in psychosis. He had worked extensively with orphans, street children, delinquents in addition to infants from where he developed many of his ideas.

7) **What is the 'True Self' and the 'False Self'?**

Winnicott discovered that a normal child lives out his childhood and then grows into maturity and leaves behind his childhood in a natural course just as we were once infatuated with toys as children but now we are not. We have naturally outgrown our liking for toys.

However if the child is not able to live out his childhood in a natural way either because economic or social circumstances force him to act mature before age or because the parents are not supportive and force the child to behave as they want him to be rather than as he would like to be or due to some other reason, then the child develops a premature and artificial layer in his psyche from where he operates to adjust to the world and escape from fear and pain. This artificial layer which actually is nothing more than a defense is what Winnicott called the False Self. The True Self which could not live itself out is hiding behind the false self to save itself.

In therapy when people come as adults with a strong false self they complain they don't feel grounded, alive and themselves. They feel artificial, being someone else all the time and some true part of them which ought to be as not existing. The task of therapy from Winnicott's standpoint is then to unmask the mask of the false self, bring it awareness, see it as a defense that is dysfunctional and dismantle it inorder to reach to the true self and then develop the true self. It is in the true self that the springs of joy, naturalness, play and aliveness are to be found, it is there that the river of life flows.

8) **What is 'going on being'?**

The child when it knows the mother or care taker is around and available feels secure, and get absorbed in play or developmental activities be it psychic or physical. Then the child needs to be left alone and be allowed to 'be' without any stimulation or intrusion from outside. This secure, comfortable state of the child where he is happily lost into his play or developmental activities was termed by Winnicott as the state of 'going on being'.

If hyper-anxious or hyper-active parents keep interfering the child's going-on-being is disturbed and he is not able to develop a strong ego (strength) and his development is negatively affected. This intrusion is infact an attack on the child's freedom and expression and a subtle attempt by the parents to make the child do what they want him to do. It interferes in the development of the True Self.

'Going on being' if allowed as should be, it leads to creation inside the psyche of calm silent and self assured psychic structure. Development of the true self, ability of genuine self expression, aliveness, creativity, wonder and being in bliss all become possible if 'going on being' is supported to live its full natural course.

9) **What is it to be 'alive'?**

For Winnicott to be alive is to be able to live out one's True Self. It is to be happy, curious, creative, playful, experience a genuine spontaneous sense of wonder and ability to reside in bliss. Being alive for Winnicott was a core concern and one of the very important goals of therapy and Psychoanalysis.

10) **What is 'organizing, unorganising and disintegration'?**

In early years of the infant's life, during the process of ego creation, there are stages where the nascent ego gets created and it dissolves and again gets recreated. This process goes on till an enduring ego comes to exist. This process of ego creation is called organizing and the process of dissolution is called unorganising.

Once the ego has been solidified in the adult then under stress if the ego cracks, it is different from unorganising and it is called disintegration. Unorganising for a healthy psyche is an enjoyable process whereas disintegration is essentially a turmoil creating, humiliating, anxiety provoking and painful process involving helplessness. Unorganising in an adult psyche is what happens when one enjoys engaging in creative work, the ego recedes in effect but structurally doesn't crack.

Those who have received 'good enough mothering' in childhood, experience unorganising as a pleasurable experience, while those who have not received 'good enough mothering' during childhood, experience unorganising almost like a disintegration with associated feelings of dread, terror, anxiety, helplessness, humiliation and pain.

11) Did Winnicott work with children?

Yes extensively. Winnicott worked with infants, children, orphans, street children and delinquent children. His extensive real life work with them led him to many of his ideas. He developed two important games, the game of Squiggle and the game of Spatula to work with children.

12) What is the game of Spatula?

Winnicott used to keep a Spatula on this table and infants when they would enter his consulting room would see it. They would look at it with wonder and try to grab it, ook at it, play with it and then throw it. Many times after throwing it they would ask for it. Such was the behavior of a normal healthy baby. Infant who had some problems were very hesitant to reach out to the Spatula and play with it. The game of Spatula gave Winnicott a window into the psyche of the infants.

13) What is a 'transitional object'?

Winnicott discovered that when the child slowly separates from the mother at the age of 3-4 (or in some cases earlier) the child develops an attachment and dependence on some **object** which resembles in some way the mother's breast or the mother or the object is something associated to the mother (may be her dress). The child keeps this object very close to him and the child gets highly disturbed if this object is lost or damaged. This object which appears in case of practically every child is what he termed as the 'transitional object'. The transitional object represents the breast or the mother and is a mid-way position between being with the mother and being completely separated from the mother. The transitional object stage is a natural developmental stage and once the child is passed this stage he naturally gives up the transitional object just as all adults have given up their childhood toys.

However if the child has taken to the transitional object a bit early and not as part of the natural developmental process but out of abandonment (as felt by the child) by the mother or care takers or out of mistreatment from others, then it is difficult for the child to give up the transitional object since it was taken to out of reasons which have not gone away in a psychic sense. Such children continue to be attached to and dependent on the transitional object for a long time, at times a life time. In therapy they have to be shown the true nature of their dependence on their transitional object (which is no longer transitional) and the roots of this dependence, to help them graduate out of this developmental fixation and arrest.

14) What does the child want the mother to do to help him develop as a healthy child?

The child wants the mother to provide him with 'good enough mothering' inorder to develop as a healthy child. This 'good enough mothering' consists of many things including,

a) The mother should be present both physically and emotionally for the child
b) The mother should take notice and be appreciative of the child to provide right mirroring
c) The mother should allow the child to be on his own even while she is in his zone of sight to enable him (the child) experience an uninterrupted going on being
d) The mother should be able to be provide a good holding environment both when she holds the child close to her and even otherwise
e) The mother should allow the child to express rage, anxiety and exploitation tendencies and yet give back the child love, warmth, smile, mirroring and positivity

15) Did Winnicott ever break boundaries of therapy?

Yes many times. Winnicott was very original and very practical and often this led to transgression of classical Psychoanalytic boundaries. Once he took a patient home for some days which is a nothing less than a scandal in classical Psychoanalytic terms. However Winnicott has never been accused of doing anything out of personal self interest, either financial or romantic, even when he crossed the boundaries.

16) In what countries is Winnicott popular in terms of his concepts and therapy?

Winnicott is popular in Britain, some parts of Europe, India and the United States.

17) How does Winnicott look at the causes of Psychosis?

Lack of good enough mothering for Winnicott was the root cause of Psychosis where the chaos of the inner-world could never be regulated in absence of a strong ego which could never be organized cohesively enough. The process of organizing and unorganising could never successfully happen and hence a stable strong ego could not be created. Ofcourse the absence of good enough mothering has consequences which can be explained in Kleinien and Freudian terms (and after Kohut even in Kohutian terms) but Winnicott didn't take to these classical explanations.

18) What does Winnicott say on the 'holding environment'?

Winnicott felt it was very important for the child to be able to express his aggression to his mother, often exploit her and yet be given a positive smile and love from the mother. The mother has to act like a good container and a positive giver who doesn't respond to aggression with aggression and exploitation with exploitation. The mother has to be an altruistic loving giver. Also the child when is anxious the mother should not get anxious and be the solid anchor which not only contains the child's anxieties but also reduces or eliminates it. This function of the mother, the care takers and the environment in general which 'holds' or contains the child's negative emotions like aggression, anxiety and so on and returns to the child positive emotions, nourishment and feelings is termed as the 'holding environment'.

If the holding environment is not good enough, the child doesn't find a good container and is constantly surrounded by (or filled with) objects with anxiety and aggression which his psyche can't manage. Over time the individual grows as a high anxiety, low ego strength individual. The failure of the holding environment can also lead to a variety of consequences based on other factors. For good psychic health a good enough holding environment is a necessity. In therapy when people come with this problem one of the tasks of therapy is to provide a good enough holding environment so that psyche can be put on the track of right developmental journey back again.

19) What does Winnicott say on the anti-social tendencies?

Anti-social tendency for Winnicott was a cry for help of individuals who did not have a stable consistent anchoring in the family. The delinquent was looking for a holding environment and a strong super ego to help him find an anchor, guidance and holding. Often there is a search and need of a 'parent with a good super-ego' and an expectation that delinquency will help one get it. Super-ego is desperate to complete its own development which has been arrested. It was essentially a cry for the good parent.

Ofcourse anti-social tendencies can also be rooted in psychopathy, perversion or rage which are different explanations then the one offered by Winnicott.

20) What is Play for Winnicott?

For Winnicott play happens in the transitional space between reality and phantasy. Play is not something limited to children, all our lives we have a need to play, the content of the play ofcourse changes as we age. Aliveness and playfulness to Winnicott are both the goals of life and therapy. Play includes play in relatedness, actual playful sport, play of words, play of creativity and so on. Play best happens in conditions of health, aliveness and happiness, the ideal metaphor being the play of life.

21) What it is it to be real?

For Winnicott, to be able to get over the false self and live from the true self is to be real. One is alive, natural, playful, creative and capable of spontaneous wonder and bliss, when one is real. Naturally this goes very close to classical philosophical concept of being authentic. However being authentic in Winnicott's work is not just an ideal of life, it is rooted in a psychological framework and operationally in an approach to therapy.

22) What was Winnicott's personal famous statement?

Winnicott had a mother who was often depressed and Winnicott used to try his best to take care of her and cheer her up. He famously once said in that context, 'To keep her alive became my living'. This perhaps was the personal anchor from where Winnicott's concern for 'being alive and playful' develops. Care takers who have to look after long term mentally ill patients can all safely use this statement.

23) Was Winnicott a happy and healthy person?

There is nothing like an innocent interest in Psychoanalysis and so Winnicott did have his pathology for which he underwent analysis twice with different analysts of different schools. However he substantially overcame his pathology and amongst all leading thinkers he was one of the most healthy, happy and alive.

24) Who are the thinkers who have taken forward the work of Winnicott?

Adam Phillips, Michael Jacobs, Michael Eigen are some of the major contributors to Winnicottian thinking.

25) What are the major resources to access on Winnicott?

Winnicott by Adam Phillips and D.W. Winnicott by Michael Jacobs are two good books to access on Winnicott. Once through it one can read Winnicott in original who unlike other analysts is easy and enjoyable to read. Lastly research papers on Winnicott and his concepts can be taken up for reading.

Tell me what you fear and I will tell you what has happened to you – Donald Winnicott

Heinz Kohut

without laughter, there would be no Tao – Lao Tzu

1) Who was Heinz Kohut?

Heinz Kohut was an American psychoanalyst who founded a school of Psychoanalysis called the Self Psychology School or the Kohutian School.

2) Why was he called Mr. Psychoanalysis?

Kohut used to eat drink and breathe Psychoanalysis, all the time he was involved in it and so his friends nicknamed him as Mr. Psychoanalysis

3) Did Kohut himself undergo multiple analysis?

Yes he did. He underwent analysis with two different analysts. The second analyst August Aichhorn was a close friend of Sigmund Freud.

4) Why did he have to break free from existing schools and create one of his own?

Kohut in his own analysis realized that there are a set of pathologies which he later termed as Self pathologies, that can't be treated with the classical Psychoanalytic method of interpretation.

Kohut said that there is something called the Self. The first thing that happens in his view is Self formation and if the Self is not formed rightly, the drive and object relations phenomenon that are classically discussed are going to get distorted to some measure. If it so happens then healing attempted from drive or object relations standpoint will not succeed because at the root, the problem is of Self Pathology.

Kohut believed that there is a category of patients (he himself was one) with Self pathology (many of whom are narcissistic or borderline personalities) for whom the right approach in therapy is not interpretation but empathic holding. Their pathology is not of drive mis-management but of an arrest of a natural process of development which needs empathic holding to restart again and get completed. This he realized from his own analysis and analysis of his patients.

There is a fundamental difference in therapy of narcissism between the Kohutian approach and the classical approach. In the classical approach the therapist is expected to bring to the notice of the patient his grandiosity which is rooted in regression to childhood omnipotence and is a barrier to reality adjustment. With this insight the patient is expected to give up his grandiosity, accepting the everyday normalcy of his being. Thus the moment one comes across grandiosity it has to be interpreted as infantile and unreal. However in Kohutian approach one allows the patient to be with his grandiosity without interpretation till they have lived out the grandiosity completely and then slowly with empathy a turn is taken to graduate out of this grandiosity into a healthy reality. Classical analysts criticize the Kohutian approach as being one of gratification and of providing a corrective emotional experience, both of which classical analysis doesn't allow for.

Controversy exists on whether Kohut was right in postulating a Self and its role in pathology and also whether the Self forms first and then drive related or object relations related phenomenon happen or if all these events happen simultaneously and if it is simultaneous than what takes precedence over what and how each influences the other.

5) What school in Psychoanalysis did Kohut create?
Kohut created the school of **Self Psychology** also called the Kohutian school of Psychoanalysis.

6) What are the major concepts contributed by Kohut?
Some of concepts contributed by Kohut are empathy, ego cohesion, narcissistic line of development, healthy narcissism, impingement, Self pathology, Self defect, bipolar self, mirroring, idealization, the arc of tension, self-objects, twin-ship and alter-ego.

7) How does Kohut define Self?
Kohut did not define Self though he developed his entire theory based on the central concept of the Self. Self for Kohut is something which can't be defined, but can be felt to be at work, guiding one in the process of self-actualization. Kohut's Self is not the same as Jung's self doesn't have to create itself in the developmental process. Kohut's Self is also not Winnicott's true self, the two are different, Kohut's Self has no opposite unlike in case of Winnicott where the true self has its opposite in the false self.

8) What is Self Psychology?

Self Psychology is an approach in Psychoanalysis which is different from the approach of the drive school and the object relations school. It is based on the premise that there is something called the Self, a line of development of the Self and distinct sets of Self Pathologies which are to be treated in therapy by Kohutian and not classical approach. .

9) What according to Kohut is the essential path for Self formation?

In Kohut's view the infant wants parents (or care takers) to attend to him and admire him, this is what he calls as 'mirroring'. The infant also needs parents who are such that they can be idealized by the infant and the infant can 'sink' into them and partake a part of their idealism for assimilating it in oneself. This is what he calls as Idealization. If both mirroring and idealization happen in a healthy way in an environment of empathy the infant is able to healthily undertake the journey of Self formation.

Self formation happens in two phases. In phase one the infant develops grandiose fantasies about himself and in phase two is he slowly learns reality and he gives up his grandiosity moving into a realistic position of healthy confidence. However if the infant doesn't get a good empathic holding and supportive environment, the infant is not able to complete the journey and remains fixated at the stage of grandiosity leading to a pathological narcissistic Self, coupled with low ego cohesion and difficulties in relationships.

The goal of therapy for such patients is to provide an empathic holding environment so as to restart the arrested process of Self development. The patient has to be enabled to live out his grandiosity, assimilate it into the psyche and move on to a realistic healthy Self.

10) What is Mirroring?

The infant is born with an innate exhibitionism and a desire for omnipotence. The infant as it indulges in exhibitionism (shows off his competence and resourcefulness), it expects the parents or care-takers to admire his exhibitionist actions. Attention, acceptance, validation and admiration is sought from the parents and if they give it to the child, it is called mirroring. Mirroring also includes confirming the child's self belief of grandiosity and omnipotence. If however the parents refuse to provide 'mirroring' the child is left with deep seated lasting doubts about his worth and competence. Many of such children turn out to have a narcissistic personality with its natural consequences.

In therapy the needs for mirroring comes out very explicitly in case of narcisstic and borderline patients and they have to be empathically met, in Kohut's view.

11) What is Idealization?

Apart from the need of mirroring the infant has a second need called the need for Idealization. What is means is that the child is innately predisposed to idealizing his parents and partaking some of their idealized qualities and assimilating it into himself.

For idealization to happen, parents or caretakers have to be good enough for the child to fantasize of them as being reservoirs of ideals and the child has to be constitutionally good enough not have very high envy and have capacity to assimilate the goodness of the parents. Idealization is this process whereby the infant sinks into the idealized parents or care-takers and makes his own a part of the reservoir of ideals.

If parents or care-takers are not ideal enough or if they are not present enough or if owing to some other psychic phenomenon the infant is not able to sink into the ideal reservoir a Self development difficulty arises (in Freudian terms a super-ego difficulty) in the sense the ego ideal is not strongly built.

In therapy patients with difficulties rooted in idealization, idealize the therapist and in Kohutian approach the same is allowed to work out itself without much interpretation, inorder to restart the Self development process.

12) What is a Bi-polar Self?

Self Psychology (Kohutian approach) suggests that the Self develops in a way that there are two poles. On one side is a pole of competences and ambitions and on the other side there is a pole of ideals and goals. The Self so constituted of these two poles is called the bi-polar self.

13) What is the Arc of Tension?

Arc of Tension is the tension that is created conceptually speaking between the two poles of the bi-polar self. In everyday language it would be the tension between the competence and the goal and it motivates us to enhance our competence to achieve our goals. The goals provide purpose and competences provide a sense of self worth and adventure. Our moving towards and attaining goals help us satisfy our desires, develop our capacities and realize self-fulfillment.

14) What is a Healthy Self and a Grandiose Self?

In Kohut's view the every child passes through a stage of omnipotence where it believes it is omnipotent, self sufficient, all good and eternal. This is the state of the Self where the Self is called the 'Grandiose Self'. The infant desires and actually lives out the Grandiose Self for quite some time. However over time, in the natural course of development, slow and optimum frustrations happen and the infant starts learning and accepting reality. Over a period of time the infant modifies his self image, Grandiosity is given up in favor of reality, and a realistic healthy Self is established.

However if the infant is not able to live out his grandiose self (when it ought to) then a severe inferiority sets in the infant and he develops by reaction formation a pathological Narcissistic Self. The Narcissistic Self is an outer defensive cover for a hidden inferiority and beneath this inferiority is repressed the grandiose self stays repressed.

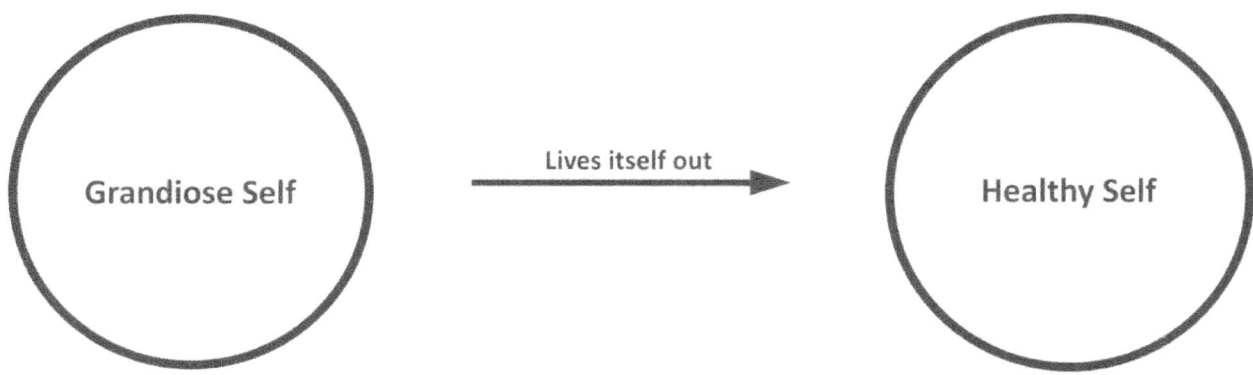

GRANDIOSE SELF TO HEALTHY SELF

GRANDIOSE SELF TO NARCISSISTIC SELF

In therapy the grandiose self is allowed to come up and live itself out and slowly the Self graduates from a grandiose self to a reality congruent Healthy Self.

15) What is Narcissism? Can there be a Healthy Narcissism?
For Kohut Narcissism is not essentially pathological, rather there is a healthy form of narcissism too. Also for Kohut every individual in the process of his Self formation passes through a stage of grandiosity and it is natural. Narcissism

develops when there is a failure in mirroring, idealization or lack of empathy on part of parents or care takers.

For Kohut the narcissistic personality is on a continuum in terms of ego cohesion (ego strength). The continuum has three types of personalities on it, the psychotic personality, the borderline personality and the narcissistic personality. The psychotic personality is the one with lowest ego cohesion and where the ego is in the state of disintegration (to different degrees) most of the times. The borderline personality has higher than the psychotic personality but not high enough to have a stable undistintegrated ego on an enduring basis. Lastly on the continuum is the narcissistic personality where ego cohesion is higher than the borderline personality and it (ego) disintegrates only occasionally.

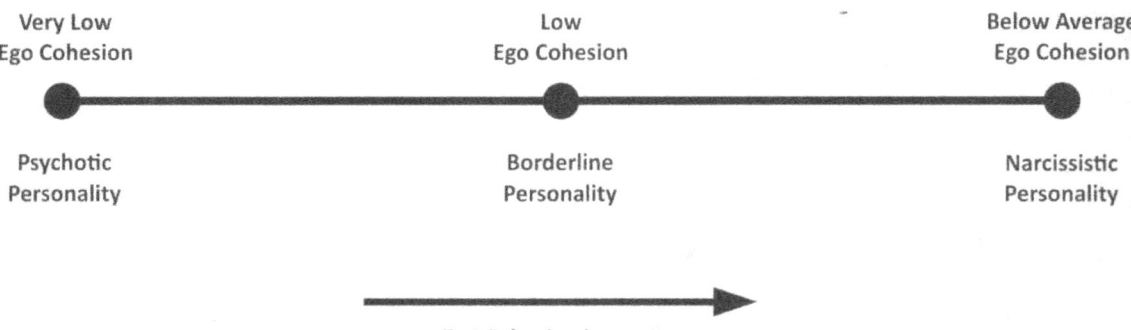

CONTINUUM OF EGO COHESION

In therapy Kohut says, it is the interpretation (criticism) of grandiosity that pushes it even deeper into the unconscious.

Unlike many psychoanalysts Kohut did that there is something called a healthy narcissism. Leaders who accomplish extra-ordinary things have quite a good amount of healthy narcissism in them. So it is not only that it is there, rather it is the cause (or one of the causes) of many a great achievements in this world.

16) What is Ego Cohesion?

Ego cohesion refers to the strength of the ego in face of an assault (trauma) or stress, either from outside or from inside. Higher the ego cohesion better is the mental health of the person. Kohut believes if mirroring, idealizing and empathy have optimally happened, the child will have high ego cohesion. Providing the child with a proper holding environment and allowing it to be himself without any recurrent intrusion (impingement) from a parent or a care-taker (almost like Winnicott's concept of going-on-being) also is necessary for high ego cohesion.

If the ego cohesion is high the ego doesn't crack in face of an assault (trauma) or stress and consequently regression doesn't happen. This in Kohut's view was the core of psychic health. It is the regression -consequent to ego disintegration (partial or total) which happens owing to low ego cohesion- that drops one in the crater of childhood psychopathology. If ego cohesion is high then even when a childhood psychopathology exists there is no regression to it, there is no getting trapped into it and one is able to lead a normal life.

There is controversy on how ego (and hence ego cohesion) develops, whether it is a small nuclear ego that develops organically into a larger stronger ego in the process of development (where cohesion would depend on its internal adhesive spread across itself) or is it that some constituent elemental entities fuse together to constitute the ego in which case the ego cohesion would depend on the joints at the boundaries and their adhesive capacity. These for the present are meta-psychological ideas awaiting rigorous engagement.

17) What promotes ego cohesion?

Right mirroring, idealization and empathy experienced in childhood along with empathic holding environment and absence of impingement, is what promotes ego cohesion.

18) What is Impingement?

Impingement is the repeated unwarranted intrusion into the child's world when it is involved in its pleasure or growth activities. It is necessary to be around the child but not intrude in to what he is doing. One has to allow the child to be and be free to do what he wants, experiment, learn and grow. In Winnicott's words it is to allow going-on-being. Impingement impedes establishment of a strong, stable and calm intra-psychic structures and leads in the end to a low ego cohesion.

19) What is Empathy?

Empathy refers to the parents or care-takers being present and understanding and not being critical of the child. Empathy is essential to provide the child with the right holding environment owing to which the child is able to institute intra-psychic structures within himself by absorbing from his environment, peace, calm, stability, positivity and creativity.

In therapy empathy means attunement of the therapist to the patient, not being critical of the patient when he exhibits his grandiose self. It also means putting oneself in the patient's shoes to understand what he is saying from inside out (his standpoint) to yield us a 360 degree comprehension of it. It also means providing the patient a peaceful, reliable and positive holding environment.

20) What is a Self-Object?

The child when he starts relating, doesn't realize that people (objects in a psychological sense) he is relating to are independent in themselves with a mind, desire and autonomy of their own. The child feels the objects are an extension of himself and that he should be able to control objects just as he controls his own hands or legs. The child realizes in small doses that his control on the objects is partial but yet there is no realization of independent objects. Thus in this stage of development the objects are not independent of the Self. The child has no concept of 'I' and 'not I'. The object at this stage appears to be an extension of the Self and hence is called a Self-object.

The Self-object is neither a part oneself completely nor completely 'the other'. At that stage of development, parents and care-takers have to behave in a way that this desire of the child of having Self-objects that satisfy his wishes to a great extent is satisfied. Only slowly thereafter reality learning has to be brought in so that the child realizes the reality that the objects are infact independent of him.

All of us have in us some degree an unsatisfied and often unlived need for Self-objects and thus in a secret way we all search for someone who would behave exactly we wish he should and work for satisfaction of our desires without any resistance.

21) What is twin-ship or and what are alter-ego needs?

Kohut believed that in childhood and often in therapy also there is a need that is seen and the need is to relate to a person as if he is an extension of oneself, almost a double. This need is called a twin-ship need and the person is termed as an alter-ego. It is a special kind of a self-object relation where there is a conscious recognition of the other object being separate in reality but in an unconscious psychic sense there is a fusion. One can see it in children at schools where if one child is slapped often the other (the friend) cries.

The term alter-ego in a separate sense in Psychoanalysis is also used to denote a person who corresponds (generally in a positive way) to the unconscious part of our self and thus in a way complements and completes our self. It is like two jig-saw puzzle parts coming together to complete a design. Alter-ego is also used in some contexts to mean some person who behaves as his master's voice.

22) What is the difference in Kohutian therapy and traditional Psychoanalytic Psychotherapy?

Kohut lays emphasis on 'holding' and 'empathy'. For him if the Self is well formed, the ego cohesion is high and if this is so, regression doesn't happen easily and with it one avoids falling into the crater of infantile psychopathologies. Thus the preventive and healing beliefs of Self Psychology are distinct.

Secondly, while traditional Psychoanalysis treats grandiosity with interpretations, the Kohutian approach is to provide holding and empathy and allow the phase of grandiosity to work out itself. Only when the grandiosity has been lived out and an ego with relatively good cohesion is available, interpretations are given. Kohut believed that offering classical interpretation to patients with Self formation issues actually pushes the grandiosity deeper into the unconscious and hence healing at the most fundamental level never happens.

Thus in the initial part of Kohutian analysis, the therapist is an empathic holding parent and not an agent of reality unlike in classical psychoanalysis.

23) In what countries is Kohutian therapy popular?

Kohut's approach is popular in the United States and is slowly getting adherents and admirers in small pockets in different parts of the world. Self Psychology is yet to be substantially assimilated into classical Psychoanalysis.

24) What are the resources for Self Psychology?

Ernst Wolf has written extensively on Kohut and he is both very good to read and highly readable. One can from here move on to Kohut in original. Self Psychology has a very good web presence and a good amount of material can be found online. Lastly research papers on Self Psychology can be read.

25) **Who are the important contributors after Kohut in Self Psychology?**
Ernest Wolf, Arnold Goldberg, Paul Stepansky, Charles Strozier, Miriam Elson, Paul Ornstein, Geoffrey cocks, Paul Toplin, Marian Toplin, F D Phillips are some of the important Kohutian thinkers who have taken extensively worked in Self Psychology.

Empathy is the capacity to think and feel oneself into the inner life of another person –

Heinz Kohut

Habib Davanloo

Tao is the eternal void filled with infinite possibilities – Lao Tzu

1. **Who is Dr Habib Davanloo?**

   Dr Habib Davanloo is a psychoanalyst who has invented ISTDP (Intensive Short Term Dynamic Therapy). Presently he is at Montreal Canada where he holds his annual seminars.

2. **What is Dr Habib Davanloo's contribution to Psychoanalysis?**

   Dr. Habib Davanloo is considered to be one of the most original recent thinkers in Psychoanalysis. Ever since psychoanalysis began there was a quest to make it affordable, swift and more structured but no one could find a way out. Dr Davanloo has solved this century old problem. He has also turned on its head many of the long held beliefs in Psychoanalysis.

3. **What is the basic concept behind his approach?**

   Davanloo in his practice as a classical psychoanalyst was in search for a more intense and short term method for analysis. Over time with the consent of the patients he started recording the sessions to discern patterns. He discovered many consistent patterns regarding the movement of resistance, optimum anxiety, excessive anxiety, movement of rage in the body, movement of anxiety in the body, the rage towards the parents, the repressed guilt and resistance to emotional closeness. Based on this he developed his method ISTDP which is based on the given insights,

   a) Human beings are instinctually attachment based creatures. However our attempts at attachment are mostly only partially successful since our parents or care givers are essentially imperfect human beings. This leads to frustration and rage for our parents and our care givers.

   b) This murderous or torturous rage causes guilt in us which leads to a series of self defeating behaviors

   c) If a person is confronted while being focused on a subject (pathology), the resistance at first increases, then it reaches a climax and then all of a sudden it drops providing a large and rapid access to the unconscious, something that is seldom seen in classical Psychoanalysis

   d) Once the murderous and torturous rage is brought out in transference or directly, guilt is felt consciously and completely. After this a range of feelings that were hidden come up and healing happens. It is almost as though the rage and guilt were a cover that used to prevent hidden feelings from surfacing.

e) We have in the deepest parts of ourselves have a desire for emotional closeness (which however we resist since over time and experience we have built an unconscious template, 'emotional closeness brings pain')

Davanloo video records his session (ofcourse with the consent of the patient) so both he and the patient can see the recording and learn from it to enhance efficacy of coming sessions.

4. **What is ISTDP all about?**

ISTDP is about doing Psychotherapy in an intensive way in a short period of time. The underlying framework is of Psychoanalysis with some sprinkling of CBT (Cognitive Behavioral therapy) and CDT (Cognitive Dynamic therapy) however in terms of technique it is a completely new way of doing therapy. It is rapidly spreading across the world that wanted the goodness and depth of Psychoanalysis without its problems of cost, time and lack of focus.

5. **What are the three phases in general of the ISTDP therapy?**

The three phases in general are Pressure, Challenge and Head-on Collision. In the first phase of pressure, the patient is made to focus on the problem he has and to arrive at a clear statement of his problem and know the fact that he has come to therapy of his own free will and is ready to do his best for healing.

The Challenge phase constitutes of two sub-phases, the clarification phase where the defense as it comes up in response to a therapist's intervention is brought to the notice of the patient and in the second sub-phase the actual challenging stance is taken to try to get closer to the hidden feeling in the unconscious.

The third phase is of Head on Collision where the therapist makes it clear to the patient that, a) the patient had voluntary sought therapy and is paying for it and b) the cost of siding with the defenses instead of the therapist, that the patient will have to pay, if he doesn't co-operate in his own healing.

With an informed, sincere and committed patient on the side of healing, one is able to move to the hidden depths of the unconscious.

6. How does ISTDP compare with classical Psychoanalysis in terms of efficacy and relapse?

   ISTDP has shown to have a better efficacy in terms of quick healing and low relapse compared to classical Psychoanalytic Psychotherapy

7. **Is ISTDP applicable to all disorders with good efficacy?**

   Yes except for a few disorders like extreme borderline cases or deeply psychotic cases or patients with very low ego strength owing to some other reasons

8. Does a patient has to have a good ego strength for ISTDP?

   Yes ISTDP does demand a good ego strength on part of the patient and so acute psychotic and borderline patients are not the right patients to be dealt with by this method. In many cases where the deficit in ego strength is not acute, the ego strength to some extent can be built over time with ISTDP.

9. **What is the normal process of healing in an ISTDP session?**

   With relentless focus on the feelings and their corresponding sensations in the body, slowly the therapist gets past defenses to the hidden feelings. Most often at this stage, the murderous and torturous rage towards parents comes out leading to a feeling of guilt. Once past this stage, a range of feelings come up allowing an easy assimilation of unconscious material which for long was hidden.

   In the above process an important aspect involved is the release of affect (hidden feelings) into the striated muscles. This is what at the roots results in healing. If the said affect instead of moving into striated muscles would have moved into the soft muscles, it would have led to psycho-somatic problems. On the other hand if the said affect would have moved into neither of the muscles and would have continued to be in the complex, the pathology would have continued.

10. How long are ISTDP therapy sessions?

    The first session is usually of 3 hours and thereafter sessions are usually of 1.5 hours or 3 hours.

11. **Does ISTDP therapy happen lying on a couch? How long does ISTDP therapy go on?**

    No it is done face to face, the session being video recorded. While Psychoanalysis talks of years, ISTDP talks of weeks and months. Generally it is a few months that ISTDP therapy should take.

12. Are all ISTDP sessions video recorded?

Yes they are unless the patient specifically requests not to for some acceptable reason. Not recording is not generally an option, rather sharing it with someone or not is always an option. If the patient so wishes, it is seen then only by the patient and the therapist.

13. What is murderous rage and torturous rage?

Davanloo states that we are all attachment driven individuals and early in life we get attached to our parents or our care givers. However our expectations as children are of having all good, all giving perfect omnipotent parents (or care givers). Naturally these expectations are bound to be frustrated and that creates in us a murderous rage and a torturous rage towards our parents or care givers. Some people may have only murderous rage but not torturous rage. Torturous rage is deeper than the murderous rage.

14. What is guilt and self destructive behavior according to ISTDP?

The presence of murderous rage and torturous rage in us towards the parents or care givers, creates an intense guilt in us because these are the very people we love intensely too. The guilt leads us to punishing ourselves mostly by our self destructive behavior and it doesn't allow us to live happily and as successfully as we otherwise have the potential to. Once the rage is made aware and lived out in therapy and related guilt fully experienced, this self destructive behavior is overcome and a new aliveness is experienced.

15. What is 'feeling' as it is dealt with in therapy?

Usually when we say 'I am angry' we are using the word 'anger' to express a feeling or a collection of feelings which are present in us at that time. However we don't really express how we are 'feeling' the emotion 'anger' in more constituent emotional terms or in terms of sensations in the body. In ISTDP therapy the focus is to 'fully feel' the feeling with full awareness. The therapist has to take the patient from a state where he just uses a word for a feeling to his fully 'feeling' the feeling which involves articulation of the complete psychological aspect of feeling and corresponding feeling in the body. ISTDP doesn't allow 'our getting away with words' when it comes to feelings.

16. What is the concept of affect moving into striated muscles and soft muscles?

Davanloo observes that affect can be released in the body into both the striated muscles and the soft muscles. Affect in healthy conditions should normally move into the striated muscles. However under repression and force of vicissitudes affect starts moving into the soft muscles causing psychological and psycho-somatic problems. The task of therapy hence is to rechannelise the flow of affect from the soft muscles to the striated muscles.

17. Is the murderous and torturous rage experienced in therapy in transference?

Yes in most cases, it is so. The transference on to the therapist means the rage is projected onto the therapist and the patient in fantasy commits torture or murder or both of the therapist. Later as therapy progresses he realizes that it was transference and actually he was doing it not to the therapist but to his parents or care givers.

18. Why do we always take this route of uncovering murderous and torturous rage, then on to guilt? How does this lead to an overall healing and well-being?

We take this route, because most people have this rage in them and for most people uncovering this rage and the guilt behind it (and self destructive behavior owing to this guilt) is very important to deal with. It leads to reduction in self defeating behavior, an enhanced self awareness, enhanced ego strength, a vivid feeling of being alive and an emotional openness to relate, denoting healing and well-being.

19. How is ISTDP different from classical Psychoanalysis?

ISTDP is based on face to face therapy which is video recorded and it involves often a direct confrontation with the patient. ISTDP sessions can vary from 45 minutes to 3 hours. The first session usually is of three hours. More than one ISTDP sessions can be taken per day though generally it is avoided. All of this is completely different from classical Psychoanalysis. Some common entities between the two therapies are fundamental concepts related to the unconscious, affect, defenses, attachment and object relations. The techniques of the two therapies are completely different.

20. Is it necessary to know Psychoanalysis before moving into ISTDP as a therapist?

Ideally Yes, because it uses the fundamental concepts of Psychoanalysis, however if someone was to say that he could learn basics in two years and then take to ISTDP without becoming a certified psychoanalyst, yes it is perfectly possible. I believe there would be certified ISTDP therapists who have not had psychoanalytic training.

21. What is triangle of conflict?

The triangle of conflict was first suggested by H Ezriel. The triangle of feeling, defense and anxiety is called the triangle of conflict. The idea is that when a difficult feeling is present in the unconscious and you try to approach it, there is anxiety and a defense comes in to reduce the anxiety and to push the feeling back deeper into the unconscious.

In therapy when the therapist tries to allow the hidden feelings to come up, the patient generally responds with anxiety or a defense which the therapist has to recognize and help the patient work through

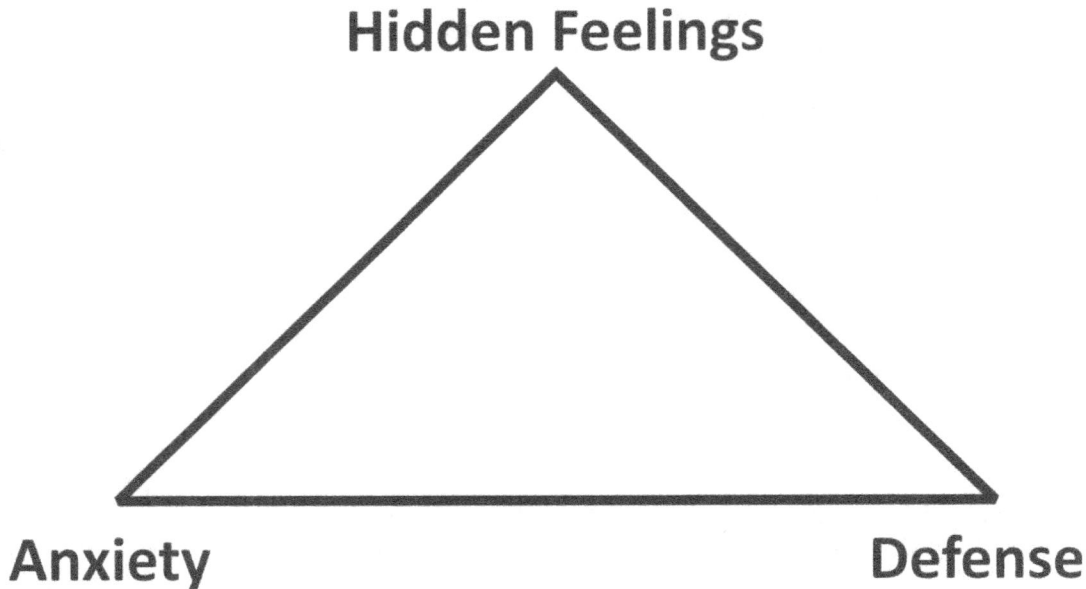

TRIANGLE OF CONFLICT

22. What is triangle of persons?

The triangle of persons refers to the triangle involving the parent, the therapist and others. It is of great use in understanding how pathological psychic patterns developed unconsciously in dealing with parents and the same are re-created in relating with the therapist and others in society. The triangle of persons was first proposed by Menninger. Dr Malan popularized both the triangle of conflict and the triangle of persons. Both triangles are extensively used by therapists for ISTDP. The therapist has to show to the patient the triangle of persons at work in his case and the dysfunctional psychic functioning it can lead to.

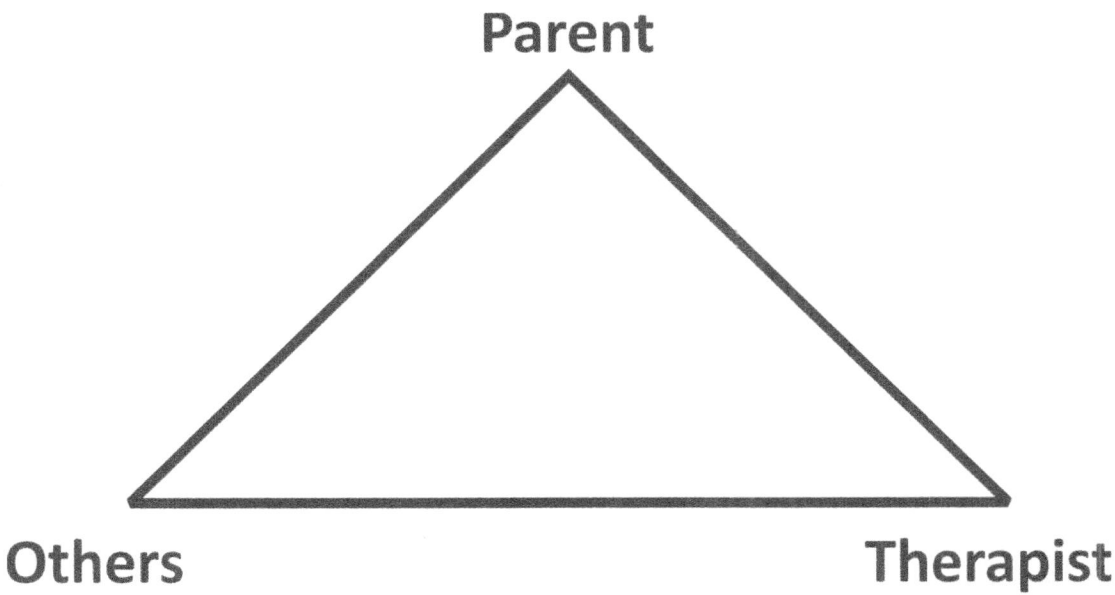

Parent

Others   **Therapist**

TRIANGLE OF PERSONS

23. What happens when anxiety becomes too high to bear?

When anxiety becomes too high to bear it can result in loss of muscle tone, falling listless posture of the body or in severe cases cognitive perceptual disturbances. The therapist has to ensure that the patient is kept in an optimum anxiety zone where work can be done and the patient is not unbearably overwhelmed with anxiety resulting in foresaid difficulties. Often when the therapist sees rising anxiety he stops further exploration of feelings and changes the conversation to the fact that as he spoke about certain issues or feelings, the anxiety showed a rise. If the patient is able to be aware of it and see this relation, his anxiety gets regulated and his ego strength is enhanced.

24. How do you know you are operating within tolerable anxiety?

The tone of the body muscle, absence of cognitive perceptual disturbances, absence of any psycho-somatic symptom and often a strong sigh or a strong solid voice indicate there is still capacity to take anxiety and that we are within the tolerable zone. Over a period of time every therapist develops his repertoire of signs on how to make out if we are in the tolerable anxiety zone. If the anxiety is going beyond the tolerable limits the therapist slows down to regulate anxiety and if the anxiety is within the tolerable zone, the therapist continues to push to access the hidden feelings in the unconscious and dismantling the defenses that come in the way.

25. How does ISTDP deal with resistance which prevents the access to the unconscious feelings?

ISTDP uses a variety of ways to overcome resistance that prevents access to the unconscious. Some of the measures used are,

a) Unwavering focus on dismantling defenses and if necessary confrontation

b) Bringing to the notice of the patient the cost he pays by being with the defense and not with the therapist, converting the pathology into something that is ego dystonic

c) Focusing on feelings as they are felt in the body and a relentless focus on repressed anger that ultimately leads to murderous and torturous rage towards parents or care takers

26. Do people feel sensations of energy, heat, buildup of a vortex like feeling etc. in different parts of the body during ISTDP?

Yes it has been extensively documented that very specific feelings at very specific parts of the body are felt during ISTDP. This comes very close to ancient Indian and Chinese ideas on there being an energy circulatory system in the body on lines of a blood circulatory system and that there are emotional and energy centers in the body.

27. Does ISTDP combine useful elements from CBT and Psychoanalysis as also from other therapies?

Yes it does. It draws both in spirit and in letter ideas from CBT (Cognitive Behavioral therapy) and CDT (Cognitive Dynamic therapy)

28. How do I become an ISTDP therapist?

Please visit the ISTDP institute website for this. There are short duration introductory programmes and if you feel interested you can enroll for the 'core programme' which is a 3 year programme and it trains you to become an ISTDP therapist.

29. Who are the leading ISTDP theorists and practitioners today?

Davanloo the founder of ISTDP is now at Canada and he holds a seminar every year to share his latest thinking on developing ISTDP further. Apart from him, the leading theorists and practitioners of ISTDP at present include; Alan Abbass, D Malan, Jon Frederickson, Tom Brod, Patricia Coughlin Della Selva and J Worchel.

30. What are the resources I can access to learn more about ISTDP?

The website of ISTDP institute is the best source. The website has written material and educational videos by the best of practitioners in ISTDF. One can begin with books by Jon Frederickson and Patricia Coughlin Della Selva and then move on to read Davanloo in original. Past this one can take to research papers on ISTDP especially by Davanloo or by Alan Abass.

the greatest resistance people show, is the resistance to emotional closeness –
Habib Davanloo

Should I go for Psychoanalytic Psychotherapy?

knowing others is wisdom, knowing yourself is Enlightenment - Lao Tzu

This section addresses issues that would be of interest if you or someone close to you is considering going for Psychoanalytic Psychotherapy.

1. **What is the concept of 'lines of defense'?**

   Like in case of biological health in the area of psychological health also there are preventive measures and healing measures. Within healing measures there are short term and long term measures.

   You don't solve a problem with a battle tank if you can solve with a hammer. Thus if you have a soft psychological problem you can go for a short term counseling or therapy. You may just take a strip of tablets and after one strip of tablets get well and forget about it. However if the short term therapies don't work and you are advised to take pills for a long duration then in such cases one should go for a long term therapy like Psychoanalytic Psychotherapy.

   These healing options constitute the 'lines of defense'. The first line of defense is a good and happy lifestyle. The second line of defense is counseling. The third line of defense is a strip of tablets. The fourth line of defense is short term therapies like CBT or ISTDP and the fifth and last line of defense is long term therapies like Psychoanalytic Psychotherapy. Often you may have to work on multiple lines (say medication and long term therapy) of defense simultaneously if the situation so is.

2) **Is there a Patient – Problem –Pathy congruence?**

   Yes there is though no one says it. There are patients who respond to one type of therapy much better than to another type. Say in the conservative society in India where people grow up being told what to do, prescriptive therapies like CBT are much closer to the culture and often work better than Psychoanalysis which depends on freedom, personal honesty, individualism and thinking out for oneself. (doesn't mean there isn't a constituency in India which responds better to Psychoanalytic Psychotherapy)

   Similarly there are certain pathologies which respond better to certain therapies, I would list out two of them, Narcissistic pathologies respond much better to Kohutian therapy and pathologies which are accompanied by Psycho-Somatic diseases respond much better to ISTDP.

The difficulty is given the complexity of the issue nobody has been able to come out and create consensus on a patient-problem-pathy grid which is so much a need of the hour to stop people wasting time and money and keep needlessly suffering by helping them start off with an optimum treatment plan.

3) **Are all people equally disposed to benefit from Psychoanalytic Psychotherapy or does personality matter?**

Personality like culture does matter. Not everyone can benefit equally from every type of therapy. There is definitely a person-problem-therapy fit. Although no Psychotherapy will admit it, every Psychotherapy has its strengths and weakness and its fitness for a particular type of individual or otherwise. You have to choose a therapy that suits you. First step is to go for short term therapies and if it doesn't work then go for long term therapies. Deeper and stronger are the roots of the problem, more long term and deeper therapies one has to choose.

Within Psychoanalysis itself 'believers' often find Jungian therapy better compared to the classical Freudian or Kleinien therapies. Those with problems rooted in the first three years of life find Kleinien therapy or Mahlerian approach much beneficial compared to those whose problems are rooted in 3.5-7 years (range) of age who often find Freudian approach more rewarding. Again, those with narcissistic issues find Kohutian approach more suited whereas those who have no obvious pathology but who have a search for meaning may find something like Logo therapy more beneficial and may even go outside the circle of Psychoanalysis. So each to his own, you have to find your therapy in consultation with an honest psychotherapist.

4) Should I go for Psychoanalytic Psychotherapy?

If you have a problem, that is rooted in early childhood and is located in your unconscious. And if you are open to exploring yourself, see the difficult parts of yourself, not hold back in discussing even embarrassing parts of yourself and if you have a readiness to feel uncomfortable feelings of guilt, shame and so on then you are the right person to benefit from Psychoanalytic Psychotherapy. You can however start with a short term therapy like CBT or ISTDP and in case they don't heal, one can go for a long term (and costly) therapy like Psychoanalytic Psychotherapy.

5) **What should I beware of if I go for Psychoanalytic Psychotherapy?**

One should be aware of not getting addicted to Psychotherapy, not developing too much dependency (irreversible) on the therapist and always remember life has to be lived outside the therapy room and not inside. Therapy room has to be the healing space and not the living space.

6) **Can Psychoanalytic Psychotherapy become an addiction I am not able to break off later?**

Yes in some cases (rare though) it happens that the patient becomes addicted to therapy and the empathic uncritical listening that one gets in therapy. The person then reduces interacting with people in the outside world and talks (and tries to live) more with the therapist. Such patients also often develop a dependence on the therapist and are unable to terminate the therapy which then becomes almost like an addiction. In some cases the patient out of transference or otherwise develops a strong desire to be in a relationship with the therapist and that again adds to the addiction part.

7) **Can you change the analyst in Psychoanalytic Psychotherapy?**

Yes you can but it is to be done only after deep deliberation and a consultation with the analyst you are with and also the one you wish to go to. It should be taken recourse to only if no progress is seen in analysis despite long analysis. In some cases it can be owing to contingent conditions like if the therapist is found to be short on ethics or if your ability to pay fees goes down or either you or the therapist is moving out to a different city.

8) **Can you change the school of Psychoanalytic Psychotherapy?**

Yes you can but do it only after a deep deliberation and talking to your analyst and if necessary taking independent opinion from two or three other analysts. However it should be done only in extreme cases where despite long therapy no healing or progress is seen.

Many of the famed psychoanalysts like Guntrip and Bion had undergone two analysis under two different analysts practicing different schools of Psychoanalysis.

9) **Can Psychoanalytic Psychotherapy be problem focused?**

Psychoanalytic Psychotherapy is always focused on healing unlike Psychoanalysis which is wide and open. However even further if a micro focus is needed, one can have a sharply problem focused Psychoanalytic Psychotherapy

10) **Does every therapist actually go to a supervisor? Is confidentiality maintained there?**

Yes every therapist has to have a supervisor. He may not discuss every case and every session but the therapist has to have atleast occasional discussion with the supervisor. Confidentiality is definitely maintained there since even when the therapist discusses a session or a case with the supervisor, the identity of the patient is kept secret and the supervisor never knows whose case or session is being discussed.

11) Is there Freud Worship or Klein Worship found in Psychoanalysis?

Yes there is an abundance of it, you have devotees even in the temple of reason. Every school of Psychoanalysis has become a military camp eager to defend itself and attack the other. The spirit of accommodation and enrichment by synthesis is not easy to find in Psychoanalysis. The price is often paid by Psychoanalysis and by patients. In academic publications, even today it is not easy to get a research paper published without quoting the masters (peace be upon them).

12) How open or closed is this discipline?

It is as closed or open as any other academic discipline. Every discipline has its own gods and worship of the false gods and Psychoanalysis is no exception. It is true that there is now openness in the journals and in discourse, a much different state than what it was 25 years back. However even today it is not easy to publish a paper without paying religious homage to the founding fathers of the schools in Psychoanalysis. I think the openness is being driven by both the thinkers inside Psychoanalysis and the environment which is increasingly becoming eclectic and open not only in the sense of inter-school synthesis but also in the sense of being open to synthesis of Psychoanalysis with holistic alternative healing modalities like Reiki or Pranic Healing. Regardless of what practitioners say or do, the patients have already become eclectic.

13) Who are the ones who need Psychoanalytic Psychotherapy but never come to it?

Quite a substantial number (not all) of people who are sincere members of religious or mystical groups actually need therapy. However owing to fear and resistance they avoid therapy and join the religious or mystical groups in hope of a miraculous cure. Many who take to crime are also those who are in need of therapy but who never come for it. There is also a large group of people on Psychiatric medication who stands to benefit from therapy but they never seek it since their Psychiatrist is not in favor of therapy. Lastly there are those who don't know of 'therapy' or those who can't afford it don't come to therapy.

14) How much is the patient responsible for success or failure of therapy?

The patient is largely responsible for success or failure of therapy. Unless the patient actually does free association, opens up oneself honestly, accepts the right interpretation and is open to relating to the therapist, healing can hardly happen. The patient also has to take insight of therapy to life outside and put insights into practice there and institute and consolidate gains for real healing to happen.

15) Why people drop out of therapy?

There can be many reasons, for some it may be cost or time, for some it may be the inability to see the difficult parts of oneself and for some it may be a genuine non-realization of results.

16) Is it true that going into therapy can trigger latent neurosis of psychosis?

In general it doesn't happen, only in rare cases does a latent neurosis or psychosis is triggered and if it happens, the therapist gets from an interpretative mode to a supportive mode to help the patient slowly build ego strength after which therapy can safely begin again. However If the psyche is such that ego strength can't be built then it has to be a long supportive therapy with conservative estimates for healing but for such patients it is often the best possible. Some acutely borderline or fragile narcissistic patients show this phenomenon.

17) Do you for sure get healed with Psychoanalytic Psychotherapy?

Everyone who goes to a doctor doesn't get healed that doesn't mean you don't go to a doctor. The same is true of Psychoanalytic Psychotherapy. Most people who come do experience healing to different degrees and there would be some who don't get any results. However those who don't benefit at all are rare, most people do benefit.

18) Does Psychoanalytic Psychotherapist force you into an orientation of Individualism which is difficult to practice in Asian societies?

It is true that Psychoanalysis is rooted in Individualism and not Collectivism. The therapy doesn't force you to adopt individualism. However it is true that most people leave therapy being more individualistic then they were when they came into therapy. In Asian societies people after therapy generally find a 'safe middle zone' to live inorder to adjust with the main-stream society. Those who can't adjust to the society at all, do have an adjustment problem and they generally find small groups sharing their beliefs to associate with. In extremely conservative societies like the Arab societies it is indeed true that coming out of therapy is not easy since there is no 'safe middle zone'.

19) Do you start succumbing to the therapist's views as you continue with therapy?

It may be in the beginning that as the transference happens and the therapist becomes the omnipotent parent, the patient may look for mirroring or acceptance or confirmation. However as the therapy proceeds and healing happens, the patient discovers his authentic preferences and makes his own choices without succumbing to anyone's views, neither of the therapist nor of anyone else.

20) Are Psychoanalysts happy and successful people in their personal lives?

Most therapists are better in the therapy room than outside. In many cities therapists keep their social circle limited mostly to other therapists and many therapists are not able to hold long term stable happy relationships. The divorce rate amongst therapists is high by any standards. Easy to heal, than to live.

21) Do psychoanalysts live incestuous social lives within their professional circuits?

Yes it is largely true especially in developing countries that most psychoanalysts have the same circle for professional and personal lives and there is in a metaphorical sense, an incestuous life

22) What kind of people choose to become Psychoanalysts?

There have been many studies in the area of occupational psychology trying to understand what type of people choose what type of profession and why. In case of Psychotherapy it has been found that a great percentage of people who opted for this profession had a narcissistic personality, depressive personality or a personality with a very strong child or a parent.

I believe apart from the motivation to genuinely help others which ofcourse is there, there are also unconscious motivations of voyeurism, filling up one's loneliness, narcissistic desire of respect without reason, unfulfilled sexual and relationship desires, the authority position and a privilege to offer wisdom. All these unconscious motivations also play a role in the choice of the profession of psychotherapists. In some cases the therapist himself has unresolved psychological issues (ofcourse not so serious that he can't be a therapist) and in some rare cases some physical problem which inclines him to a job of a therapist which needs minimum of physical exertion and can be practiced till late in life.

23) Do most Psychoanalysts have adequate 'width of life experience' ?

Some have it and some don't. Those who don't have it often make too theoretical or off mark judgments or interpretations. These are also the ones who tend to be more puritan, self righteous and inflexible. Those that have adequate width of life experience generally are more flexible and are sought after by patients who professionally are business men or politicians.

24) **Is Psychoanalysis a new religion, a new priesthood professing solutions to the problems of living?**

Critics have indeed criticized it as such. The therapist like a priest gives judgments in the forms of interpretations. The Psychoanalytic theory is the new holy book by the standards of which the 'normalcy' is to be judged. The therapist is the omnipotent father figure to whom no questions can be asked. The technique and axioms as given by the founding fathers of the schools are absolute and it is heresy to question them and every different opinion is a resistance. The imperfections of the theory and its inability of empirical validation are glossed over, a new faith has been instituted. Such indeed is the criticism from critics.

However there are some stark differences also between Psychoanalysis and religion. Psychoanalysis doesn't have any value system to propound either pro faith or anti faith. It is open to experimentation and peer review. Every two decades we have major advances and revisions in theory and most importantly every therapist in his training undergoes a personal experience and validation of the fundamental concepts of Psychoanalysis. Lastly as neurology advances and empirical evaluation of Psychoanalysis becomes increasingly possible, Psychoanalysis will get a more scientific foundation. Psychoanalysis is eager to enter the laboratory, religion is terrified of it.

25) **Is Psychoanalytic Psychotherapy covered by Insurance?**

No unfortunately as of now it is not covered by Insurance in most countries. Short term goal oriented therapies like CBT are covered by Insurance and may be shortly ISTDP may also be covered, however the long term and open ended nature of Psychoanalytic Psychotherapy makes it difficult to be covered by Insurance in most countries.

26) **Can one combine alternative healing techniques like Reiki, Pranic Healing, Tai chi, acupressure and others with Psychoanalytic Psychotherapy?**

In an official sense no but with holistic healing making rapid progress and with its increasing acceptance, many patients now also go for alternative healing practices along with Psychotherapy. Especially relaxation driven alternative healing systems like Reiki and Hypnotherapy are widely taken to by patients today. On the part of the therapist classical

Psychoanalytic Psychotherapists don't recommend any additional therapy classical or alternative.

27) Can we take five most common everyday events we come across and explain them with Psychoanalysis?

Let us take the five everyday events,

I) Change in Habits post death of a loved one

Often after the death of a loved one you will observe the person (who has lost the loved one) will develop some of the habits or traits of the lost person. This in Psychoanalytic terms is the unconscious defense of 'denial'. By doing what the departed person used to do, you deny that he is no more since the activity is happening. It is a way the psyche copes up with the loss.

II) Avoidance of celebrity or successful people

Some people (not all) can't see interviews, stage performances or felicitations of celebrities who currently are at the peak of their careers. It is owing to their narcissism (in Psychoanalytic terms) that they inwardly feel they are equal or more talented and therefore equally or more deserving of prosperity and fame. This gives rise in them to intense feelings of anger and envy (both of which are extremely uncomfortable to control and bear) which leads them to avoidance of celebrities or successful people. Often they also indulge in irrational criticism of the successful to take out their anger and envy and 'cut them to size'.

III) Fear of boss

In Psychoanalytic terms the boss represents the father figure, the authority figure and many people have an out of proportion fear of the boss which psychoanalytically is the pathological fear of the father figure. It is also true that at times, it is not direct fear of the power of the authority figure but that there is a murderous or torturous anger towards the authority figures and the person projects it on to the boss and then unconsciously feels (unconsciously ofcourse) the boss is going to torture or kill him and hence is full of anxiety. Ofcourse all these are unconscious phenomenon and one is not aware of.

IV) People thronging to see a celebrity

People when they throng crazy to see a celebrity or to shake hands or to touch the celebrity are infact trying to get close to their own narcissism which they have projected on to the celebrity. The narcissistic self image of all good, all beautiful, all admired, all famous, immortal and omnipotent is projected on the celebrity. The hero worship is secretly a self worship of one's narcissistic self image projected on the object of worship.

V) To have or not to have, good possessions?

Many people don't find it easy to buy good things or maintain them even though they have enough money and also a desire to have and enjoy these things. There is a strange tendency not have these things which opposes very silently and mostly in a non-decisive weak way the desire to have these things.

Say for an example, you want to buy a new car but you keep postponing it. You buy it at last however every time you drive it you feel anxious and you feel very happy when a friend takes the car away for a few days. (such is in fact the case for many people)

Psychoanalytically this is explained as the fear that something will happen to the object you love either because of yourself or because of someone else. This is rooted in your infantile attacks on the good breast and your feelings of abandonment by good objects and your experience of some objects you loved getting hurt, damaged or destroyed.

Thus you want good objects (the car) but every time you drive it, unconsciously you fear that you will destroy it in an accident or someone else will hurt or damage it and when that happens a catastrophe will happen and unbearable feelings (of fear, pain, inferiority, destitution, loss) will arise. To avoid such unbearable feelings, you avoid driving the car. When a friend requests you to give him your car for a few days, secretly you feel very happy (apart from the happiness you feel for helping a friend) that you won't destroy the car, nor will someone else and that the unbearable feelings will not arise. This 'feel good' continues for some time and if the car doesn't come back for a long time again, you feel loss of the good object. Thus there is a paradox you live of wanting a good object and fearing that something will happen to it, trying to keep it at distance and avoiding the loss of it.

There are two main hazards of Psychoanalysis; that it might fail and that if it succeeds -
Mignon McLaughlin

Some common Psycho-Pathological Issues
And their Psychoanalytic Explanation

Tao called Tao is not Tao – Lao Tzu

1. Paranoia

There are two Psychoanalytic explanations of paranoia one based on the Freudian approach and the second based on the Klienien approach.

The Freudian explanation is based on repressed homosexuality. The person who has strong repressed homosexuality feels attracted homosexually to somebody but it is not acceptable to his morality and so in his unconscious mind, from a position of 'I love you' he goes to the position of 'I hate you' (through a psychological defense of reaction formation) and then it intensifies over time to a position of 'I will kill you' however again this position being unacceptable to his morality, he disowns his desire to kill the other and instead attributes the same to the other person saying the other person wants to kill him (by a psychological defense of projection). This belief that the other person is out there to kill him then creates the anxiety that the attack will happen any moment. This anxiety is what leads to paranoia.

The Kleinien explanation is that the infant who has destroyed the bad breast fears that the bad breast has not been completely destroyed and so it will come back to take revenge and attack the infant with even more ferocity and 'torturous and murderous' intent than what the infant did to it. This fear of the bad breast coming back to attack is what is the cause of paranoia.

Needless to say all Psychoanalytic explanations are referring to unconscious psychic operations of which the person has no awareness that they are happening in him. It is also safe to say that every explanation fits a few patients (it is from such patients that these explanations have come up in the first place) and one has to find the right explanation (from many contending explanations) for the right patient.

2. Depression

Depression in Freudian terms is understood as 'anger turned inwards' which in extreme cases can lead to suicide. The Freudian explanation of Depression is that it results from a 'loss of ambivalently cathected narcisstic object'.

What it means is that if you relate to any person such that the person does more or less as you wish to him to do and that for such a person you have simultaneous love and hate (ofcourse in different proportions) then loss of such a person in your life happens, then it can lead to depression.

The process is that when a loss of such a person happens, we are not able to let go the memory of the person or the feelings associated with him. We hence make the person and feelings associated with him, a part of our self. Here all feelings we had towards the person (including anger) now are turned inwards towards our self since the lost person is not a part of our self. Such 'anger turned inwards', leads to depression. In simple words depression is anger towards someone or something turned onto oneself. If this anger was to be expressed completely or released in some other way, depression would be healed.

Some people (some Freudians and some non-Freudians) also believe that the loss of a person or object or situation brings sadness which can lead to depression without involvement of anger. Just the amount of sadness is so much that one is not able to feel and release it and is captured and fixated into it. If depression is so understood then the healing process then acquires a different route.

This is only one explanation of depression. In fact for every psychological problem, every school of Psychoanalysis has its own explanation and a way of healing. What works for you is the best explanation for you.

In Kleinien terms, Depression can happen when there is loss of the all good breast. One of the Kleiniens (hope I can say so) Bion used to say 'where there was a nipple, now there is a hole', the hole leads into Depression.

Some analysts would also point out that in many cases it is just 'anger' against someone (mostly an authority figure) that not being expressed, accumulates and leads to depression. With such an explanation, no ambivalent relationship or loss of good breast is necessary, a real life situation involving simple repression or suppression is enough to lead to depression.

3. **Phobia**

Phobia is displacement of fear. An innocent object or situation becomes a dreaded object or situation because fear from somewhere else is displaced on to the innocent object or situation. The fear that is displaced can come from in Freudian view from the castration anxiety or the fear of committing the Oedipal or incest transgression.

4. Suicide

Suicide is anger turned inwards at its extreme. It is explained by the phenomenon that when one loses an object with whom one shared an ambivalent love-hate relationship and the object was narcissistic object choice (near to Kohut's self-object) one is not able to detach feelings of love and anger which are bound up with the object and so normal mourning and grief don't happen. Instead the lost object is taken into the psyche and made a part of it and the anger towards the object hence now is directed towards oneself. This anger (extreme) turned inwards leads one to suicide.

Ofcourse there can be suicides of helplessness and a situation of 'no way out' where no Psychoanalytic explanations are necessary or valid.

5. **Mania**

Mania is a state of a high where the normal inhibitions go away and one experiences heightened state of happiness, an unrealistic assessment of one's ability and a new found freedom of expression. In Freudian terms this happens when the fantasy and reality become one and one regresses to his infant narcissistic state of omnipotence and unalloyed happiness and bliss. In process terms, when the energy damned up in depression or anxiety suddenly is found free it takes one back to the state of narcissistic omnipotence of childhood. The dream and reality becoming one, mania ensues.

Some Freudians also believe Mania is the exhilaration of realizing the desires of the Oedipus complex and a temporary suspension of reality where a free ID flows out suspending the EGO.

In Klienien terms some would say, it happens when one finds or becomes one with the omnipotent good breast which has (or is) all good with all the richness of the world. This archaic merger of one's ego (or some would say the Self) into the all good breast leads one to the exhilaration or ecstasy of Mania.

6. Stammering

Stammering is related to fear of the authority figures, it is essentially a castration anxiety in the Freudian terms. In object relations approach it can also be, owing to fear of attack of the bad breast. Attachment theorists would say it is the fear of 'assault', 'pain' and the fear of object (and attachment) loss that leads to stammering. The Ego schools would say it is the fear of attack (on) and disintegration (of) the ego and fear of pain (of ego loss or humiliation) that leads to stammering.

7. **Success Avoidance (Self defeating behavior)**

In Freudian terms for people who have not been able to resolve their Oedipus complex, becoming successful is equivalent to killing the father in the unconscious which is highly guilt provoking and so many people who are otherwise capable and deserving avoid success (ofcourse in unconscious ways) and leadership roles.

Some people don't avoid success completely and do become successful, but just after they succeed in something or are felicitated, they feel depressed because in the unconscious they have killed their father. It (unconscious success avoidance) is also called success neurosis.

8. **The dance of intimacy**

Some people play this dance of intimacy in relationships. When you go near they try to maintain distance and when you go far they try to come near you. Such people always try to operate in a zone that is a 'safe zone' for them. The Psychoanalytic explanation of this dance of intimacy is that such people are operating on the fusion-abandonment continuum. When they get intimate they fear fusion with the object of love because with fusion comes annihilation, and when you go far they fear abandonment which also brings in annihilation. The annihilation anxiety operates both ways and such people keep playing the dance of intimacy with underlying dynamic of fusion-abandonment phenomenon.

9. **Greed**

The infant in early years especially in anal phase feels his feces are an act of his creativity and something very valuable he doesn't wish to part with and wishes to collect it. Those obsessed with greed have not been able to resolve the issues of their anal stage of collecting feces. This is a Freudian explanation.

The second explanation Klienien explanation is that the infant feels the good breast has all the richness of the world into it and the infant feels envy and narcissistic rage that he doesn't have that richness and he has to be dependent on the good breast. The infant hence feels intense greed to rob off the good breast of all its riches. This infantile wish to have and hoard all the richness of the good breast is the underlying dynamic for greed.

10. Compulsive Washing of Hands

The Psychoanalytic explanation is that it is an act of washing off ones guilt, the guilt of having committed or intending to commit an Oedipal crime, incest crime, killing or torture of an early attachment figure, in the unconscious.

11. Ceaseless Prayers

Some people have the habit of praying ceaselessly across the day or playing prayers on their music player and they feel if they don't do it something bad will happen. It is rooted in catastrophic thinking and that inturn is rooted in the anxiety that the oedipal or incest crime will happen (Freudian explanation) or that the bad breast will attack (the Klienien explanation)

12. Catastrophic thinking

Catastrophic thinking is rooted Psychoanalytically speaking in the anxiety that the oedipal or incest crime (the catastrophe) will happen and with it at times is also the fear that castration will happen, all of which is rooted in a desire to commit the crime which is floating in the unconscious. Such is the Freudian explanation.

The Klienien explanation is that any time the attack of the bad breast (the catastrophe) can happen or that the loss of the good breast (the catastrophe) can happen.

Some who are more into attachment theory would say the catastrophe is actually the catastrophe of abandonment and the unconscious fear s that abandonment will happen leading to annihilation anxiety and unbearable pain.

13. Preparation for Genocide

Politicians or Religious leaders when they are preparing ground for a mass genocide, in Psychoanalytic terms they have to make their people project their unacceptable parts (shadow in Jungian terms) from the unconscious onto those who are to be killed. Once the projection happens, the other seems all evil (the Kleinien (all) bad breast, not a mixture of good and evil that we all are). Once someone appears all evil, its killing stands justified.

14. Parents who delay marriage and accelerate divorce

Many parents who otherwise have no financial or social constraints don't work sincerely towards marriage of their children (and this is more applicable to traditional societies where parents have a substantial role to play in marriage) however after marriage if something goes wrong they (parents) are extremely active and energetic in encouraging divorce. Psychoanalytically such parents are extremely emotionally insecure from within and are strongly bonded to their children and they don't want to lose them so they try to delay marriage and hasten divorce. Often along with fear of abandonment (which is triggered in them the moment children get into marriage) there is often a strong reverse Oedipal or incest desire in the unconscious.

15. Can't work with a Target

Some people can produce excellent results when not given a target but when given a target they are not able to achieve half of what they achieved in the same time and resources when they were not given a target. The Psychoanalytic explanation is that such people have an intense castration anxiety, catastrophic thinking and an inferiority complex that leads them to a crippling anxiety the moment targets are given due to which they are not able to perform.

Mental health problems do not affect three or four out of every five persons but one out of one. - William Menninger

Resources on Psychoanalysis

a. Books

1) Introduction to Psychoanalysis – by Brenner
2) New Introductory lectures on Psychoanalysis - by Sigmund Freud
3) Interpretation of Dreams – by Sigmund Freud
4) Sigmund Freud -Past Masters series by Oxford Publications – by Anthony Storr
5) Psychology of the Unconscious – by Carl Jung
6) Man and his symbols – by Carl Jung
7) Carl Jung – Past Masters series by Oxford Publications – by Anthony Stevens
8) Introduction to the work of Melanie Klein – by Hanna Segal
9) Psychoanalysis of Children – by Melanie Klein
10) Envy and Gratitude – by Melanie Klein
11) Elements of Psychoanalysis – by Wilfred Bion
12) Experiences in Groups – by Wilfred Bion
13) Clinical thinking of Wilfred Bion- by Neville Symington
14) Human Nature – by Donald Winnicott
15) Playing and Reality – by Donald Winnicott
16) Through Pediatrics to Psychoanalysis: Collected Papers – by Donald Winnicott
17) The analysis of the Self –by Heinz Kohut
18) The restoration of the Self – by Heinz Kohut
19) Treating the Self : Elements of Self Psychology – by Ernest Wolf
20) Intensive Short-Term Dynamic Psychotherapy – by Patricia Coughlin Della Selva
21) Lives Transformed : A Revolutionary method of Dynamic Psychotherapy – by David Malan and Patricia Coughlin Della Selva
22) Co-creating Change: Effective Dynamic Therapy Techniques – by Jon Frederickson

b. Websites

1) https://en.wikipedia.org/wiki/Sigmund_Freud
2) www.iep.utm.edu/freud
3) www.bbc.co.uk/history/historic_figures/freud_sigmund.shtml
4) https://en.wikipedia.org/wiki/Melanie_Klein
5) www.melanie-klein-trust.org.uk/
6) https://en.wikipedia.org/wiki/Wilfred_Bion
7) https://en.wikipedia.org/wiki/Donald_Winnicott
8) https://en.wikipedia.org/wiki/Heinz_Kohut
9) www.selfpsychology.com/
10) http://www.selfpsychologyPsychoanalysis.org/
11) www.istdp.com
12) istdpinstitute.com

c. Videos

1. https://www.youtube.com/watch?v=G7juouc7vbo
2. https://www.youtube.com/watch?v=3ySsLRwE3Lk
3. https://www.youtube.com/watch?v=mQaqXK7z9LM
4. https://www.youtube.com/watch?v=_sm5YFnEPBE
5. https://www.youtube.com/watch?v=HU3iSW6WTo8
6. https://www.youtube.com/watch?v=jlsxqqgkw88
7. https://www.youtube.com/watch?v=v90H5UTJHoY
8. https://www.youtube.com/watch?v=kAPyRryK1HY
9. https://www.youtube.com/watch?v=lViOY9wIDBQ
10. https://www.youtube.com/watch?v=eLJsiQ4h3fY
11. https://www.youtube.com/watch?v=O67a8_XXqK4
12. https://www.youtube.com/watch?v=r68oInRsFEI
13. https://www.youtube.com/watch?v=oDab093cPPc
14. https://www.youtube.com/watch?v=ZaZkvvB367I
15. https://www.youtube.com/watch?v=v90H5UTJHoY
16. https://www.youtube.com/watch?v=RBFjreZsnn4
17. https://www.youtube.com/watch?v=ZQ6Y3hoKI8U
18. https://www.youtube.com/watch?v=f4A2BudUKHs
19. https://www.youtube.com/watch?v=UJlVCzKM_gA
20. https://www.youtube.com/watch?v=cKzmk2-xnzY
21. https://www.youtube.com/watch?v=22yLR49VUeM

about the author

Himanshu Vaidya is management consultant, trainer, teacher and a psychotherapist. He has written and spoken on a variety of issues ranging from management, philosophy, psychoanalysis, history, politics and spirituality. His present interests are focused on culture and synthesis of paradigms on the Self.

He teaches a course on 'Psychoanalysis and Philosophy' and offers training programmes in Psychoanalysis, Dream Analysis, Brand Management, Corporate Social Responsibility and Non-Profit Management.

He works extensively in the non-profit area and contributes especially through his non-profit organization 'Brick Foundation' which is focused on areas of mental health, education and social enterprise development.

write to the author at, hvindia@gmail.com

Disclaimer: Any resemblance of any character or event dealt with in the book to any real person or institution is purely incidental and no intention exists to refer to any real person or institution so as to cause any harm or injury to anyone.

CREDITS: GREEN ORANGE PVT. LTD FOR GRAPHICS

www.ingramcontent.com/pod-product-compliance
Lightning Source LLC
Chambersburg PA
CBHW081148280526
45787CB00008B/3258